Whispers of the Soul:
A Poetry Anthology on Mental Health and Well-being

Ismael S. Rodriguez Jr. 365 Northwest 43rd Court Oakland Park, FL 33309

https://thebulletproofpoet1.godaddysites.com/home

Whispers of the Soul: A Poetry Anthology on Mental Health and Well-being / Ismael S. Rodriguez Jr.

Table of Contents

Introduction: Whispers of the Soul - A Poetry Anthology on Mental Health and Well-being

In the quiet spaces between words, where syllables linger like echoes, we discover a sanctuary—a refuge for the soul to unfold, unravel, and resonate. Welcome to "Whispers of the Soul," an anthology crafted with delicate intentionality, seeking to traverse the landscapes of mental health, self-care, and the profound journey toward well-being.

Within this tapestry of human existence, emotions weave a complex narrative. Yet, amidst the vibrant threads of joy, sorrow, and longing, there exists an often overlooked, yet profoundly significant realm: mental health. It is here that our inner battles unfold—the silent struggles, the hidden scars, and the resilience that blooms even in the darkest corners of our hearts.

"Whispers of the Soul" invites you to embark on a poetic odyssey. Together, we navigate intricate pathways—the delicate balance between vulnerability and strength, the rhythm of healing, and the power of shared stories. Each verse becomes a lantern, illuminating the way toward acceptance, compassion, and self-discovery.

So let us listen closely to these whispered truths, for within them lies the promise of understanding, connection, and hope. May this anthology be a balm for weary hearts, a testament to the resilience of the human spirit, and a reminder that even in shadows, light finds its way.

Why Poetry?

Poetry, with its lyrical brevity and metaphorical resonance, possesses an innate ability to articulate the ineffable depths of human emotion. It is a language that speaks directly to the heart, transcending the limitations of conventional dialogue by delving into the subtle nuances of our shared experiences. Through carefully crafted verses, poetry serves as a conduit for expressing the complexities of mental health, shedding light on the shadows that often cloak our inner struggles. In its artful arrangement of words, poetry invites readers to embark on a journey of introspection and empathy, fostering a deeper understanding of the human condition and the profound intricacies of the mind.

In the anthology, each poem serves as a poignant reminder of the interconnectedness of our collective humanity, offering solace and companionship to those grappling with mental health challenges. Through metaphor and symbolism, poets can illuminate the path towards healing and hope, casting light on the resilience that resides within each individual. By embracing vulnerability and embracing the transformative power of self-expression, these verses pave the way for meaningful dialogue and mutual support. Ultimately, poetry becomes not only a means of artistic expression but also a beacon of compassion, bridging the divide between silence and understanding in the realm of mental health.

Sections That Echo the Human Spirit

Within the pages of my anthology, the intricacies of the human spirit unfold through carefully curated sections, each reflecting a facet of our collective journey towards mental health and well-being. "Embracing Vulnerability" marks the inaugural step, beckoning readers to bravely confront the raw authenticity found within their vulnerabilities, acknowledging them as the bedrock of genuine human connection. Transitioning into "The Dark Night of the Soul," the anthology delves into the shadows of despair and uncertainty, affirming the resilience that allows individuals to navigate through even the most profound emotional depths without succumbing to darkness.

As the anthology progresses, "Healing and Hope" emerges as a guiding light, illuminating the transformative power of resilience and the innate capacity for renewal within the human spirit. Through introspective verses, readers are invited to witness the journey towards emotional restoration and rediscover hope amidst adversity. In contrast, "Self-Care Rituals" offers a tender celebration of the seemingly mundane yet profoundly impactful acts of self-nurturance that contribute to holistic well-being, emphasizing the importance of intentional care for the mind, body, and soul.

The subsequent sections—"Mind-Body Connection," "Seeking Support," "Stigma and Breaking Barriers," and "The Beauty of Imperfection"—form a vibrant mosaic of collective expression, transcending individual narratives to weave a universal tapestry of understanding and compassion. Here, the anthology becomes a sanctuary where diverse voices converge, offering insights into the interwoven complexities of the human experience and fostering empathy in the shared journey towards mental wellness. As readers traverse through each section, they bear witness to the resilience, vulnerability, and inherent beauty that define our shared humanity, finding solace and inspiration within the transformative power of poetry.

A Collective Conversation

Within these pages, I bear witness to the intricacies and depths of the human mind, inviting readers to embark on an immersive journey through the labyrinth of mental health. "Whispers of the Soul" isn't merely a collection of verses; it's an open invitation—an exploration into the uncharted territories of our emotional landscapes. Here, amidst the lines and stanzas, words become more than mere ink on paper; they transform into bridges, spanning the chasms between experiences, perspectives, and emotions. This anthology isn't a prescription for healing but rather a sanctuary—a space where vulnerability is honored, where voices resonate with authenticity, and where the complexities of mental health find their voice in verse.

As you turn the pages of "Whispers of the Soul," may you find solace in the shared humanity that permeates each poem. Within these lines, may you discover echoes of your own struggles, reflections of your triumphs, and reminders that your journey is intertwined with countless others. Together, let us peel back the layers of stigma and silence, embracing the beauty found in vulnerability and the strength derived from solidarity. Through the transformative power of poetry, let us navigate the winding paths of self-discovery, resilience, and renewal. Let the whispers of the soul guide you through these pages, weaving a tapestry of understanding, compassion, and hope in the tapestry of our collective experience.

Let the whispers of the soul guide you through these pages.

With heartfelt words,

Ismael S Rodriguez Jr

Section 1: Embracing Vulnerability

In Section 1 of "Whispers of the Soul: A Poetry Anthology on Mental Health and Well-being," Ismael S. Rodriguez Jr. emerges as a poignant voice, capturing the essence of embracing vulnerability amidst the tumult of mental health challenges. Through his evocative verses, Ismael fearlessly delves into the depths of human emotion, inviting readers into a world where vulnerability is not a weakness but a source of profound strength. His poems resonate with authenticity, offering solace to those grappling with their inner struggles, and illuminating the path towards self-acceptance and healing.

In Ismael's verses, vulnerability becomes a transformative force, breaking down barriers and forging genuine connections between individuals. Through his introspective exploration, he highlights the beauty in embracing one's flaws and imperfections, recognizing them as integral parts of the human experience. Ismael's poetry serves as a reminder that vulnerability is not synonymous with defeat but rather a testament to the resilience of the human spirit. In Section 1, readers are encouraged to confront their vulnerabilities with courage and compassion, finding strength in their shared humanity and the power of poetic expression.

Naked Truths

In the quiet chamber of the heart,
    Where shadows dance and secrets start,
    There lies a place, untamed, unseen,
    Where naked truths unveil the sheen.
    Beneath the layers we've carefully spun,
    A tapestry of battles fought and won,
    There echoes a voice, raw and true,
    Yearning to break the silence through.
    Naked truths, stripped of pretense,
    Whispers of vulnerability commence,
    A sacred unveiling, courage in bloom,
    As we step into the sacred room.
    In the mirror of introspection,
    Reflections of our imperfection,
    Each flaw, a stroke in life's design,
    A testament to the strength we find.
    The world may crave a polished facade,
    But within, a tempest, a river broad,
    For in vulnerability, we find the key,
    To unlock the shackles and set hearts free.
    Confessions etched in ink's embrace,
    Words cascading with unbridled grace,
    A cathartic dance of pen on page,
    Releasing the captive soul from its cage.
    Courage, a flame in the darkest night,
    Illuminating corners, banishing fright,
    For in the act of baring one's soul,
    A healing journey begins to unroll.
    Beneath the surface, a tempest brews,
    A symphony of emotions, varied hues,

From the quietest whispers to the loudest roars,
A waterfall of feelings, crashing shores.
Cracked vessels, worn by the tide,
Yet within those fractures, strength abides,
For vulnerability is not a sign of defeat,
But a hymn sung by hearts, resilient and sweet.
In the arms of vulnerability, we find,
A sanctuary for the restless mind,
A place where masks are gently shed,
And the authenticity of self is spread.
Whispers of insecurity, soft and low,
Echoes of doubt that often grow,
Yet in acknowledgment, they lose their might,
Fading into the embracing light.
Transparent soul, crystal clear,
A mirror reflecting what we hold dear,
For in the rawness of an unveiled core,
Lies the beauty that we're searching for.
Unveiled scars, stories etched in skin,
Narratives of battles fought within,
Each mark, a testament, a badge of grace,
A roadmap to navigate life's intricate space.
Dancing with shadows, an intimate affair,
A choreography of self-aware,
For vulnerability is not a waltz alone,
But a dance with shadows, yet to be known.
So let the naked truths unfurl,
A banner of courage, a transformative swirl,
For in embracing vulnerabilities untold,
We discover strength, pure and bold.

Confessions in Ink

In the quiet sanctuary of midnight's hush,
    Where shadows dance in a clandestine rush,
    A solitary figure with a pen in hand,
    Embarks upon a journey, emotions to withstand.
    Confessions in ink, an intimate affair,
    Words poured forth, laid bare with care.
    On the canvas of paper, secrets unfold,
    A tapestry of truths, a story to be told.
    In the ink-stained chamber of a restless mind,
    Echoes of turmoil, echoes entwined.
    Unspoken fears, like ghosts, take flight,
    Exposed in verses, seeking solace in the night.
    The pen becomes a confidant, a silent friend,
    A witness to the battles no one comprehends.
    In the alchemy of verses, pain transforms,
    An elixir of healing, as the poet performs.
    Each stroke of the pen, a cathartic release,
    A therapeutic voyage, granting inner peace.
    Through the labyrinth of emotions, the poet treads,
    Weaving a tapestry of thoughts, dreams, and threads.
    Confessions in ink, a sacred pact,
    With the parchment as witness, the poet acts.
    The paper, a mirror reflecting the soul,
    As vulnerabilities and truths begin to unroll.
    The pen glides smoothly, an extension of the heart,
    Navigating realms where shadows depart.
    Ink becomes an elixir, a balm for the soul,
    A testament to the strength of being whole.
    Confessions in ink, like a phoenix's flight,
    Rising from ashes, embracing the light.

A metamorphosis in the writer's hand,
As pain transforms into a landscape grand.
So, in the silent hours when the world is asleep,
And the moon's soft glow secrets vigilantly keep,
Confessions in ink, an eloquent spree,
A whispered soliloquy, setting emotions free.

Courageous Unveiling

In the quiet corridors of the soul,
Where shadows whisper and secrets stroll,
There lies a tale, untold, unseen,
Of a heart's journey, vast and serene.
A soul, veiled in the cloak of night,
Longing to break free, take its flight.
Through corridors of silence, it weaves,
A tapestry of dreams, where courage conceives.
A tapestry of dreams, where courage conceives,
A symphony of whispers, where the heart believes,
In the power of words, in the strength to share,
The burdens within, the weight of despair.
In the hushed embrace of vulnerability,
A dance begins, a courageous unveiling spree.
Each step, a declaration, a fearless stride,
Against the current of shame, where emotions hide.
Against the current of shame, where emotions hide,
A metamorphosis unfolds, like the rising tide.
Confessions bloom like flowers in spring,
As the heart unfurls, a courageous wing.
As the heart unfurls, a courageous wing,
A phoenix rising, ready to sing.
Of battles fought in the chambers of the soul,
Of scars turned into stories, making the broken whole.
In the tapestry of vulnerability, threads intertwine,
Creating a mosaic, unique and divine.
Courageous hearts, like stars in the night,
Illuminate the darkness, embrace the light.
Illuminate the darkness, embrace the light,
For vulnerability is not a weakness, but a sight.

Into the depths, the soul fearlessly dives,
In the courageous unveiling of our lives.
So let the echoes of truth resound,
In the courageous unveiling, strength is found.
For in the silence of vulnerability, we stand tall,
Embracing imperfections, unveiling our all.

Beneath the Surface

Beneath the surface, where shadows play,
In the caverns of the heart's intricate ballet,
Lies a realm unseen, a vast expanse,
Where the dance of emotions takes its chance.
A mosaic of feelings, a palette of hues,
Painted on the canvas of life, the daily news,
Yet beneath the surface, a current flows,
A river of secrets that nobody knows.
In the quiet spaces where echoes reside,
Whispers of joy and sorrows coincide,
Beneath the surface, where the heart beats,
Lies a symphony of triumphs and defeats.
A tapestry woven with threads of fear,
Threads of hope, threads drawing near,
In the silence between each heartbeat's thud,
Resides the essence of humanity's blood.
There, vulnerability stands in full bloom,
A garden of truths, a sweet perfume,
Roots that delve into the soil of the soul,
Where authenticity takes its mighty toll.
Beneath the surface, where masks are shed,
Lies the raw truth, the core widespread,
A vulnerability that's not a sign of weakness,
But a testament to the heart's uniqueness.
For in this depth, where honesty lies,
The strength of authenticity truly flies,
Through the cracks and fractures that appear,
Emerges a spirit both brave and clear.
The scars of battles, both lost and won,
Tell tales of resilience under the sun,

Beneath the surface, where wounds may heal,
Sprouts the wisdom that time can reveal.
Dive into the abyss, brave and bold,
Where the story of a lifetime is told,
In the quiet chambers of the soul's embrace,
Beneath the surface, find your sacred space.

Cracked Vessels

In the quiet chambers of the soul,
Where shadows linger and secrets stroll,
There lies a vessel, cracked and worn,
A testament to the battles borne.
Upon its surface, etched with strife,
The scars of living, the wounds of life,
Yet within those fractures, a story unfolds,
Of resilience untold, of strength that molds.
A vessel, once whole, pristine and bright,
Now bears the marks of the endless night,
Each crack, a chapter, a line, a verse,
A testament to the universe.
For life has sculpted its masterpiece,
In the brokenness, the pain, the release,
And as the vessel stands weathered and scarred,
It holds a beauty that's not marred.
Cracks are not flaws, but tales to tell,
Of storms weathered and waves that swell,
In each fracture, a whispered plea,
To embrace the imperfections and just be.
The vessel's journey, a dance with time,
A rhythm composed in prose and rhyme,
With every fracture, it finds its song,
A melody of healing, echoing strong.
Oh, cracked vessel, bear your grace,
Show the world the lines on your face,
For in those fractures, a truth is held,
That strength emerges when hearts have swelled.
Through the shattered glass of yesteryears,
A kaleidoscope of joy appears,

The fractured vessel, a mosaic of light,
Illuminating the depths of the night.
So let the light shine through the cracks,
In broken vessels, strength relaxes,
For in the fractures, love resides,
A testament to how the heart abides.
In the quiet chambers of the soul,
Where resilience and stories stroll,
A vessel stands, cracked and free,
A symbol of the strength to be.

In the Arms of Vulnerability

In the quiet chambers of the heart's embrace,
Where shadows blend with the light's soft grace,
There lies a realm seldom ventured, rarely known,
In the arms of vulnerability, a sanctuary is grown.
A canvas painted in hues of raw emotion,
Where truths unfold, a tender, sacred potion.
Naked, unadorned, the soul stands bare,
In vulnerability's haven, no one shall despair.
Upon this stage, courage takes its stand,
A dance of hearts, entwined hand in hand.
No masks to hide, no walls to shield,
Only the authenticity of that vulnerability was revealed.
The air is thick with whispers of the unseen,
A symphony of truths, a cleansing serene.
Here, vulnerability is not a sign of defeat,
But a proclamation of strength, a heartbeat.
In this sanctuary, secrets lose their weight,
As burdens transform to feathers, elevate.
No judgment here, just understanding's gaze,
In vulnerability's embrace, a healing phase.
The scars, once hidden, now proudly worn,
Each a testament to battles fought and won.
For in vulnerability's tender hold,
Imperfections become silver threads of gold.
A river of tears flows freely, unconfined,
Washing away the echoes of the troubled mind.
A cathartic rainfall, washing the spirit clean,
In the arms of vulnerability, a rebirth unseen.
No need for armor, no need for disguise,
Here, authenticity is the most prized.

A gentle surrender to the ebb and flow,
In vulnerability's arms, true strength does grow.
Oh, how the heart beats with a rhythm pure,
In this haven where authenticity is the cure.
The vulnerability, once feared, becomes a friend,
A companion on the journey, from start to end.
So let us dwell in this sacred space,
Where vulnerability wears a gentle grace.
For it is here, beneath the moon's soft tranquility,
We find our solace in the arms of vulnerability.

Whispers of Insecurity

In the quiet chamber of the soul, where shadows dwell,
A symphony of whispers, tales untold, begin to swell.
Soft echoes of insecurities, like ghostly zephyrs, roam,
Whispering secrets, fragile dreams, in the sacred catacomb.
In the hallowed corridors of the heart's fragile keep,
The murmurs of doubt and uncertainty slowly seep.
A clandestine gathering of fears, in shadows they conspire,
To douse the flame of confidence, to kindle doubt's cold fire.
Oh, the delicate dance of insecurity's ballet,
A pirouette of shadows in the light of day.
They weave through the tapestry of the mind's terrain,
A silent waltz of whispers, an unspoken refrain.
In the mirror's gaze, reflections distort and bend,
As doubts parade in masquerade, veiled to amend.
Each flaw magnified, a distorted lens they wear,
Convincing the spirit it's marred beyond repair.
Yet, let us not dismiss these whispers out of hand,
For in their tender cadence, courage takes its stand.
To confront the fragility, the vulnerabilities we share,
Is to embark on a journey, a testament to care.
For every hushed murmur, every subtle doubt,
It is but a call for empathy, a plea to cast love's route.
To wrap our souls in understanding, in kindness unconfined,
To nurture the wounded spirit, a balm for the troubled mind.
Insecurity, a transient guest in the mansion of the self,
Begs not for dismissal but for acknowledgment and stealth.
To recognize its presence, to face it eye to eye,
Is to unravel the knots of fear, to bid the shadows goodbye.
So let the whispers echo, let them ebb and flow,
But let the response be strength, let self-compassion grow.

In the tender embrace of vulnerability's plea,
Find the courage to be imperfect, to let the soul roam free.
For in the whispers of insecurity, a paradox lies,
A call to authenticity, where the true self never hides.
So, dance amidst the whispers, with resilience be crowned,
And in the gentle whispers, let self-love be found.

Transparent Soul

In the quiet realm of introspection's gaze,
A soul unveiled, in translucent haze.
Beneath the skin, where shadows dance,
A symphony of truths, a fragile trance.
Transparent soul, a vessel pure,
In every fracture, stories endure.
Crystal-clear echoes of joy and strife,
A living canvas, the tapestry of life.
Within the chambers, secrets reside,
Unspoken whispers, nowhere to hide.
Bearing witness to the ebb and flow,
Of highs and lows, the tides that grow.
In the crucible of vulnerability,
A metamorphosis, a silent plea.
Layers shed, illusions fade,
As the essence bared, begins to cascade.
The heart, an open manuscript,
In the script of love, emotions are equipped.
Through prisms of courage, colors unfold,
A spectrum of feelings, both young and old.
Transparent soul, bathed in moonlight,
Casting shadows that dance in the night.
A kaleidoscope of dreams and fears,
A constellation of joys and tears.
In the crucible of self-revelation,
A transparent soul finds liberation.
No need for masks, no need to feign,
Authenticity reigns, breaking every chain.
Through the looking glass of introspection,
A journey unfolds, a deep connection.

With every nuance, every hue,
The transparent soul embraces what's true.
Yet, vulnerability is no sign of weakness,
But a testament to strength's uniqueness.
For in the unveiling, there's a sacred grace,
A portrait painted with courage and trace.
So let the sunlight pierce the glass,
Illuminate the shadows, as they amass.
For in transparency, we find the key,
To unlock the essence of what it means to be free.
In the silent chapel of self-discovery,
The transparent soul uncovers the mystery.
A sacred journey, an ongoing scroll,
In the epic tale of the transparent soul.

Unveiled Scars

In the tapestry of time, woven with threads unseen,
Lie stories untold, veiled in shadows serene.
Beneath the cloak of silence, where whispers reside,
Unveiled scars speak, the heart's truest guide.
Each scar, a testament etched on the soul,
A tale of battles fought, of struggles to be whole.
Gentle lines on the canvas of a life well-worn,
In the symphony of healing, a melody is born.
Unveiled scars, like ancient manuscripts unfold,
Chapters of resilience, stories yet untold.
They shimmer with echoes of tears long dried,
Yet in their unveiling, strength is implied.
Upon the tapestry, where pain leaves its mark,
A roadmap of survival, a journey through the dark.
Unseen battles waged beneath a stoic guise,
Yet each scar narrates, in hushed whispers, the cries.
In the garden of wounds, blooms courage anew,
Petals of endurance, in shades of vibrant hue.
For every scar, a badge of honor worn,
A testament to the light through shadows borne.
Oh, the beauty found in scars unveiled,
A sanctuary for the heart, where truth is exhaled.
No longer concealed, but proudly displayed,
A testament to the strength that can't be swayed.
Trace the lines with fingers, like Braille for the soul,
Feel the resilience that makes brokenness whole.
Unveiled scars, not marks of defeat,
But symbols of triumph, where pain and healing meet.
So let the scars speak, in a language unsaid,
Of battles survived, of storms weathered and shed.

For in the unveiling, we find the strength we seek,
In the stories of scars, where the bravest hearts speak.

Dancing with Shadows

In the stillness of the twilight's embrace,
Where daylight surrenders to the softness of grace,
A solitary figure, bathed in moonlit glow,
Begins a dance with shadows, a rhythm known to the soul.
With every step, a whisper in the breeze,
The echoes of yesteryears, the roots of the trees.
A silent waltz, the dance of the unseen,
Where shadows and light interweave, serene.
The first movement, a hesitant sway,
As the figure confronts the ghosts of yesterday.
Ephemeral memories, a cascade of tears,
Yet vulnerability blooms, conquering fears.
Through the ebon night, a delicate twirl,
A dance of introspection, a quest to unfurl.
Silhouettes of secrets, veiled in mystery,
Revealing fragments of a storied history.
A pas de deux with shadows that silently speak,
Of battles fought within, of strength at its peak.
The pirouette of courage, a leap into the unknown,
As the dancer embraces the shadows they've sown.
Moonbeams weave patterns on the stage,
A canvas of emotions, an intimate page.
The tango of sorrow, the cha-cha of glee,
Dancing with shadows, setting the spirit free.
In the ballroom of the mind, where echoes persist,
The dancer confronts shadows, a therapist.
Each step, a therapy, each turn, a release,
In the arms of vulnerability, finding inner peace.
As the nocturnal symphony plays its tune,
The dance intensifies beneath the watchful moon.

A fusion of heartbeats, a lyrical trance,

In the dance of shadows, a soul's elegant dance.

A finale unfolds, a bow to the night,

The dancer, once veiled, now bathed in moonlight.

For in embracing shadows, a metamorphosis is found,

A resilient spirit, in vulnerability, crowned.

So, dance with shadows, let the moonlight guide,

Through the labyrinth of emotions, where shadows abide.

In this nocturnal ballet, find solace and kin,

For the dance with shadows is where healing begins.

Section 2: The Dark Night of the Soul

In Section 2 of "Whispers of the Soul: A Poetry Anthology on Mental Health and Well-being," Ismael S Rodriguez Jr takes center stage as the sole poet, offering a deeply personal exploration of the "Dark Night of the Soul." Through his evocative verses, Rodriguez delves into the labyrinthine depths of mental health struggles, painting vivid portraits of despair, loneliness, and the tumultuous journey through the shadows of the mind. With raw honesty and unflinching vulnerability, his poetry pierces through the veil of silence that often shrouds discussions about mental illness, inviting readers to confront the complexities of their own inner worlds.

Ismael's poems resonate with a haunting beauty, capturing the weight of depression, anxiety, and other mental health challenges with poignant clarity. Through his words, he articulates the profound sense of isolation and the relentless battle against the darkness that many individuals face. Yet, amidst the somber hues of despair, glimmers of resilience and hope emerge, offering glimpses of light in the midst of the darkness. Section 2 serves as a testament to the transformative power of poetry as a medium for healing and catharsis, illuminating the often-unseen struggles of the soul and fostering a sense of solidarity and understanding among readers grappling with their own mental health journeys.

Descent into Shadows

In the twilight realms where shadows intertwine,
A journey begins, a descent to the divine.
Beneath the skin, where the soul doth hide,
A tale unfolds, of shadows deep and wide.
A solitary figure, cloaked in despair,
Travels through the dusk, burdened by a rare
And heavy weight, a darkness undefined,
A labyrinth of thoughts, a troubled mind.
The descent commences, a gradual slide,
Into the abyss where emotions hide.
Each step echoes with a muted plea,
As the soul unravels, longing to be free.
In the first layer of this shadowed abyss,
Whispers of doubt and shadows amiss.
A kaleidoscope of fears, vivid and wild,
The descent into shadows, like an unwinding dial.
The path grows darker, the air thick with gloom,
A symphony of sorrows begins to loom.
Tangled memories and regrets take flight,
As the traveler journeys deeper into the night.
Glimmers of starlight, once bright in the mind,
Now dim in the shadows, hard to find.
A dance of demons, haunting and cold,
As the descent continues, stories unfold.
Echoes of past wounds, wounds unhealed,
The traveler's heart by shadows concealed.
Yet, in the descent, a yearning persists,
For a glimmer of light, a hope that insists.
The second layer, a cavern of despair,
Silhouettes of dreams linger in the air.

The traveler's footsteps, heavy with strife,
Navigate a maze, the journey of life.
A chorus of sighs, the weight of the soul,
An exploration into the shadows' control.
Yet, amidst the darkness, a flicker, a spark,
A resilient spirit, emerging from the dark.
In the third layer, the shadows grow dense,
A confrontation with innermost defense.
The traveler grapples with ghosts of the past,
A battle of emotions, fierce and steadfast.
The descent into shadows, a quest for release,
A yearning for solace, a bidding for peace.
Yet, in the struggle, a resilience gleams,
As the traveler unravels the fabric of dreams.
The final layer, where shadows entwine,
A revelation emerges, a truth to define.
The descent into shadows, a journey complete,
The traveler emerges, shadows in retreat.
For in the depth of darkness, a seed was sown,
A seed of strength, in solitude grown.
The shadows may linger, but the soul is now free,
A symphony of shadows, a journey's decree.

Whispers of Despair

In the quiet corners where shadows linger,
And the weight of the world rests on fragile shoulders,
There echoes a symphony of whispers,
A haunting refrain of the soul's mournful boulders.
A solitary figure, lost in the vast expanse,
Dances with the demons that only they can see,
Silent cries paint the canvas of their existence,
As despair wraps its tendrils, a cruel decree.
The whispers of despair, soft as a zephyr's breath,
Yet they carve canyons in the landscape of the mind,
An invisible orchestra, playing a macabre sonnet,
Notes of sorrow, a haunting melody entwined.
In the caverns of the heart, where echoes reside,
The soul listens to the whispers, a tragic serenade,
Each syllable a weight, each murmur a heavy stride,
As hope's embers flicker, cast into the shade.
The moonlight weeps upon this desolate stage,
Where the heart's theater hosts a play of gloom,
Shattered dreams, like fragments on an empty page,
And the whispers of despair, a relentless loom.
Within the corridors of solitude, the echoes amplify,
Conversations with shadows, a dialogue obscure,
The walls bear witness to the tears that silently cry,
As the whispers of despair persist and endure.
A kaleidoscope of memories, fragments of the past,
A mosaic of pain, a portrait painted in despair,
Yet, within the darkness, a flicker, steadfast,
A resilience awakening, a glimmer of repair.
Oh, whispers of despair, relent your cruel song,
Let the spirit rise from the ashes, reborn,

For within the night, a resilient heart grows strong,
And the echoes shall fade, a new symphony is sworn.
In the alchemy of time, healing finds its way,
As the whispers dissipate, a dawn unfurls,
From the cocoon of despair, a spirit takes flight,
And in the embrace of hope, a wounded heart swirls.
For even in the darkest moments, the soul can mend,
As whispers of despair fade into distant air,
A phoenix rises, borne of strength to transcend,
And in the silence that follows, a melody of repair.

Lonely Echoes

In the hushed stillness of the moonlit night,
    Where shadows dance and stars ignite,
    There echoes a lonely, haunting song,
    A melody of solitude, melancholy so strong.
    Beneath the velvet canopy, a solitary soul,
    Wanders through the cosmos, a story to unfold,
    Lonely echoes resonate, a whispered symphony,
    Reverberating through the void, a cosmic epiphany.
    Each footstep, a soft imprint on the celestial dust,
    A pilgrimage through the universe, a soul entrust,
    To the vast expanse, the infinite unknown,
    Lonely echoes ripple, a cosmic undertone.
    The stars, witnesses to tales untold,
    Stories of love, of dreams, of hearts once bold,
    But in the tapestry of time, threads come undone,
    Lonely echoes linger, where once laughter had begun.
    The moon, a silent confidante in the velvet sky,
    Bathes the wanderer in its silver lullaby,
    Yet even lunar whispers cannot dispel,
    The loneliness that in the heart does dwell.
    Through nebulas and galaxies, a celestial roam,
    Lonely echoes weave through the astral loam,
    A tapestry of emotions, embroidered with stardust,
    The wanderer's journey, a cosmic thrust.
    In the quiet of space, where silence reigns,
    Lonely echoes pulsate, like celestial veins,
    An echo of heartbeats, a cosmic decree,
    That loneliness, too, is a part of the symphony.
    The black canvas of the cosmic sea,
    Painted with the hues of the soul's decree,

Lonely echoes rebound, like ripples in a pond,
A universal truth, a celestial bond.
Yet in this cosmic solitude, a realization blooms,
Loneliness, a companion in the astral gloom,
For every wanderer, lost in the cosmic sea,
Lonely echoes harmonize, a shared symphony.
The universe listens with a compassionate ear,
As lonely echoes dissipate, surrendering fear,
For in the vast expanse of the cosmic night,
Loneliness finds solace, bathed in starlight.
And as the lonely echoes fade away,
The wanderer, too, finds a brighter day,
For in the cosmic dance of solitude and grace,
Lonely echoes find their resting place.

The Tangled Mind

In the labyrinthine corridors of thought,
Where shadows dance and fears are wrought,
A tapestry of neurons weaves,
A maze of secrets that the mind conceives.
The Tangled Mind, a silent symphony,
A complex dance of synchrony,
Neurons firing in chaotic grace,
An intricate ballet in the mind's vast space.
Threads of memories intertwine,
A delicate dance, both yours and mine,
In the recesses of the mental fray,
Where the past and present hold hands and sway.
A labyrinth of dreams, hopes, and fears,
Woven into the tapestry of the years,
A kaleidoscope of emotions untold,
In the Tangled Mind, mysteries unfold.
At times, a harmony, sweet and clear,
A melody that the soul holds dear,
But, oh, the dissonance that may rise,
When the symphony of the mind denies.
Tangled knots of worry and despair,
A dense thicket, challenging to bear,
Yet within this chaos, a resilience grows,
A strength that the Tangled Mind bestows.
The siren call of anxiety's song,
A haunting tune that echoes strong,
Yet, amidst the cacophony of the mind,
A quiet whisper of hope, you may find.
The Tangled Mind, a paradox untold,
A story in every crevice, manifold,

A journey through the maze, hand in hand,
Guided by the light that inner strength can withstand.
Embrace the knots, the twists, the turns,
For in the Tangled Mind, the spirit learns,
To navigate the maze, to find reprieve,
And in the dance of thoughts, to truly believe.
So let the threads of consciousness entwine,
In the grand tapestry of the Tangled Mind,
For within its labyrinth, a beauty lies,
A testament to the strength that never dies.

Echoes of the Soul

In the caverns of the mind, where shadows dance,
And whispers of forgotten dreams perchance,
There lies a tale of sorrow and of woe,
A melody of echoes from long ago.
In the deep recesses where memories hide,
Lurk fragments of a soul, wounded inside,
Each echo a reminder, a silent scream,
Of hopes dashed and shattered, lost in the stream.
Through the corridors of time, they softly tread,
Echoes of the past, where dreams have bled,
They linger in the corners, haunting still,
A testament to the strength of human will.
Echoes of laughter, once bright and clear,
Now fade into silence, drowned in fear,
Echoes of tears, cascading down,
Lost in the darkness, never to be found.
In the labyrinth of the heart, where passions burn,
Echoes of love, a bittersweet return,
Whispers of longing, in the dead of night,
Searching for solace, in the pale moonlight.
But amidst the echoes, a flicker of light,
A glimmer of hope, shining bright,
For in the depths of despair, there lies a seed,
A promise of renewal, a chance to heed.
Through the echoes of the soul, a journey unfolds,
A tale of redemption, waiting to be told,
For every echo carries within its strain,
The power to heal, to rise again.
So let the echoes resonate, let them ring,
For in their sorrow, lies the song they sing,

A testament to the resilience of the soul,
A symphony of echoes, making us whole.
And though the echoes may fade, and darkness may fall,
Within the silence, we hear the soul's call,
A whisper of courage, a beacon of light,
Guiding us through the shadows of the night.
So let us embrace the echoes, let us embrace the pain,
For within their depths, lies the key to gain,
A symphony of echoes, a song of grace,
Echoes of the soul, in time and space.

Midnight Melancholy

In the heart of the night, where shadows linger long,
Beneath the silver moon's lament, I hear the sorrow's song.
A melody of whispered woes, a symphony of pain,
In the depths of darkness, where tears fall like rain.
Here, in the silence, where time stands still,
Midnight melancholy creeps, with a chilling, ghostly chill.
It wraps its arms around me, a cloak of endless night,
As I wander through the shadows, seeking a flicker of light.
The stars, they weep above me, their tears a gentle glow,
But in this lonely hour, their radiance seems to wane and slow.
The moon, a solemn witness, to the secrets that I keep,
A solitary sentinel, as I tread through dreams so deep.
In the corners of my mind, where shadows dance and play,
Memories of yesteryear, in shades of somber gray.
Each step a heavy burden, each breath a whispered sigh,
In the labyrinth of my thoughts, where echoes never die.
I wander through the corridors of doubt, through corridors of fear,
Haunted by the specters of the past, by whispers I can't hear.
The weight of melancholy, a burden hard to bear,
As I search for solace in the darkness, in the depths of despair.
But amidst the shadows, a glimmer starts to gleam,
A fragile ray of hope, like a long-forgotten dream.
It whispers of tomorrow, of a dawn yet to break,
And in its tender embrace, I find the strength to wake.
For even in the darkest night, there lies a spark of light,
A beacon in the shadows, shining bold and bright.
So, I'll journey through the darkness, with courage as my guide,
And embrace the midnight melancholy, as I let my spirit glide.
For in the heart of sorrow, there lies a hidden grace,
A testament to resilience, to the beauty of this place.

And as the night begins to fade, and morning starts to rise,
I'll greet the dawn with open arms, with hope in my weary eyes.
So let the midnight melancholy weave its somber spell,
For in the depths of darkness, there's a tale to tell.
Of resilience and redemption, of strength in the face of strife,
And the beauty of the human soul, in the dance of night and life.

Invisible Chains

In the quiet corners where shadows linger,
    Where sunlight struggles to breach the dark,
    There lies a place where whispers shiver,
    And the soul is bound by chains unseen, stark.
    Invisible chains, forged from doubts untold,
    Wrap around the heart with a silent hold,
    Each link woven from fears that silently grow,
    Binding the spirit, casting shadows below.
    They coil around moments, both day and night,
    Tethering dreams, choking hopes in their might,
    A weight unseen, yet heavy to bear,
    A burden that whispers of relentless despair.
    In the mirror's reflection, they cast their shade,
    Distorting the image, leaving scars that cascade,
    Invisible to the eye, yet felt deep within,
    As the spirit wrestles with battles unseen.
    They tighten with every whispered doubt,
    Every anxious thought, every fear devout,
    Constricting breath, suffocating air,
    As the soul struggles against their silent snare.
    But in the depths of darkness, a glimmer may rise,
    A spark of courage amidst tear-stained eyes,
    A voice that whispers, soft and clear,
    Breaking the silence, dispelling the fear.
    For in acknowledging the chains that bind,
    In shedding light on the shadows confined,
    There lies the power to break the hold,
    To find liberation, to be brave and bold.
    With each step forward, each tear shed free,
    The chains lose their grip, their potency,

For in the journey from darkness to light,
There's strength in the struggle, in the fight.
So let us unravel the invisible chains,
Let courage and hope be our guiding reins,
For in the depths of despair, there's a path to reclaim,
A journey of healing, of breaking the chains' claim.
Invisible they may be, but not invincible,
For the human spirit is resilient, indomitable,
And though the night may be dark, the dawn will rise,
Bringing freedom and light to weary eyes.

Echoes of Silence

In the hollow chambers of solitude's domain,
Where shadows dance in the quiet refrain,
There lies a symphony of muted sound,
Echoes of silence, profound and profound.
In the corridors of the mind, where thoughts collide,
There dwells a stillness, where secrets hide,
A world unseen, where whispers roam free,
In the depths of the soul's silent sea.
Each heartbeat's rhythm, a silent plea,
Echoes of silence, a symphony,
In the vast expanse of the midnight sky,
Where stars whisper secrets, as time passes by.
In the embrace of darkness, where dreams take flight,
Echoes of silence paint the canvas of night,
A whispering wind, a gentle sigh,
In the echoes of silence, we learn to defy.
The weight of the world, a burden to bear,
In the echoes of silence, we find solace there,
Amidst the chaos, amidst the storm,
In the echoes of silence, we find a form.
A formless presence, a lingering trace,
In the echoes of silence, we find our grace,
For in the quiet, we find our voice,
In the echoes of silence, we make our choice.
To rise above, to break the chains,
In the echoes of silence, where truth remains,
For in the silence, we find our might,
In the echoes of silence, we take flight.
Through the valleys of darkness, we journey on,
In the echoes of silence, we find the dawn,

A new beginning, a brand-new day,
In the echoes of silence, we find our way.
So let the echoes linger, let them ring,
In the echoes of silence, let us sing,
For in the silence, we find our song,
In the echoes of silence, we belong.
In the whispers of the wind, in the still of the night,
In the echoes of silence, we find our light,
A beacon of hope, a guiding star,
In the echoes of silence, no matter how far.
So let the echoes carry us, let them guide,
In the echoes of silence, we find our stride,
For in the silence, we find our truth,
In the echoes of silence, eternal youth.
So let the echoes of silence be our guide,
In the echoes of silence, let us reside,
For in the silence, we find our voice,
In the echoes of silence, we rejoice.

The Abyss of Anxiety

In the darkest chambers of the mind, there lies
    A place where shadows dance and whispers rise,
    An abyss, unfathomed, where anxieties breed,
    Where the soul's tempest finds its direst need.
    Here, in the hollows where silence screams loud,
    Echoes of worries weave a suffocating shroud,
    A labyrinth of doubts, a maze of fears,
    Where the weight of existence drips with tears.
    Each step forward feels like a plunge into void,
    Where every heartbeat is a drumbeat, deployed
    To march along the edge of sanity's brink,
    In the depths of despair, where shadows drink.
    The abyss of anxiety, a chasm so vast,
    Where the echoes of past traumas hold fast,
    And the future's uncertainty casts its cruel spell,
    Turning hopes into ashes, dreams into hell.
    In this cavern of chaos, where thoughts collide,
    The mind becomes a battleground, where demons hide,
    They whisper taunts and sow seeds of dread,
    As the soul trembles under the weight of what's unsaid.
    The air is thick with the scent of unease,
    As the heart races, caught in a relentless seize,
    Each breath a struggle, each moment a fight,
    Against the tides of terror that grip the night.
    But amidst the darkness, there flickers a light,
    A glimmer of hope in the depths of the night,
    For even in the abyss, where shadows reign,
    There's a strength within, a fire to reclaim.
    With each hesitant step, courage starts to grow,
    And the echoes of anxiety begin to slow,

For in facing the darkness, the soul finds its might,
And emerges from the abyss, into the light.
So let us not be defined by the depths we roam,
But by the courage we find to journey home,
Through the abyss of anxiety, we learn to soar,
And find the strength to rise, and fight, once more.

Ghosts of Yesterday

In the quiet corners of my mind they dwell,
Ghosts of yesterday, haunting, unseen,
Whispers of memories, casting their spell,
Echoes of moments where shadows convene.
They dance in the shadows of forgotten dreams,
Silent specters of a time now passed,
Their presence lingers in the moonlit beams,
In the corners of my mind, they're steadfast.
Each ghost a fragment of a bygone day,
A specter of joy, or a shroud of pain,
In the labyrinth of my thoughts, they stray,
A haunting chorus of loss and gain.
They whisper secrets of the past, untold,
Their voices soft, yet they pierce the night,
In the depths of my soul, their tales unfold,
As they wander through the corridors of fright.
But amidst the darkness, a glimmer of light,
A hope that shines through the veil of despair,
In the stillness of the night, I take flight,
Embracing the ghosts, with courage to spare.
For they are but echoes of what used to be,
Remnants of moments that shaped my soul,
In their presence, I find the key,
To heal the wounds, to once more feel whole.
So let them wander, these ghosts of yesterday,
For in their whispers, I find release,
In the depths of my being, they'll forever stay,
A testament to the journey, the path to peace.

Shadows of the Mind

In the silent depths where shadows roam,
Amid the corridors of the mind's dark home,
There lies a realm of whispers, unseen,
Where shadows dance, where fears convene.
Within the labyrinth of tangled thought,
Where echoes linger, where dreams are caught,
The shadows of the mind begin to sway,
In the crevices where light gives way.
They twist and turn, elusive, profound,
Casting veils of doubt all around,
Cloaking hopes in a shroud of gray,
In the shadows where worries stray.
In the quiet corners where secrets hide,
And in the depths where fears reside,
The shadows of the mind take flight,
In the dimness of the soul's long night.
But amidst the darkness, a flicker gleams,
A beacon of hope in the land of dreams,
For even in shadows, there lies a spark,
A glimmer of light within the dark.
So let us brave the shadows' embrace,
And seek the light in the hidden space,
For in the depths where shadows reside,
There's beauty in the journey, where fears collide.
In the dance of shadows, we find our truth,
In the whispers of darkness, the wisdom of youth,
For it's in the shadows that we learn to see,
The light that shines within you and me.

Section 3: Healing and Hope

In Section 3 of "Whispers of the Soul: A Poetry Anthology on Mental Health and Well-being," Ismael S Rodriguez Jr takes center stage as the sole poet, weaving a tapestry of verses that resonate deeply with the human experience of healing and hope amidst mental health challenges. Through his evocative poetry, Rodriguez invites readers on a transformative journey, guiding them through the labyrinth of emotional turmoil towards the light of resilience and renewal. His verses echo with the universal themes of overcoming adversity, finding solace in vulnerability, and embracing the inherent strength within oneself. With each carefully crafted stanza, Rodriguez captures the essence of the healing process, illuminating the path towards inner peace and emotional restoration.

In Ismael's poems, we encounter poignant reflections on the complexities of the human psyche, each verse a testament to the indomitable spirit that perseveres in the face of darkness. Through imagery rich with symbolism and raw emotional depth, he illustrates the cathartic power of self-expression and the catharsis found in embracing one's vulnerabilities. From the depths of despair emerge threads of hope, woven into the fabric of his poetry with delicate precision. Rodriguez's words serve as a beacon of light in the tumultuous sea of mental health struggles, offering solace and reassurance to those navigating their own journey towards well-being. As the heart and soul of Section 3, Ismael S Rodriguez Jr's poetry stands as a testament to the resilience of the human spirit and the transformative power of art in nurturing the mind, body, and soul.

Phoenix Rising

In the heart of the deepest night,
Where shadows dance and fears take flight,
A silent ember begins to ignite,
Beneath the cloak of starry light.
From the ashes of a shattered dream,
A phoenix stirs, a silent scream,
In the depths where sorrows gleam,
A fiery spirit begins to beam.
Through the trials of endless night,
Through the storms that dim the light,
Through the battles waged in spite,
A phoenix rises, burning bright.
With wings of courage, it takes flight,
In the face of darkness, it finds its might,
Through the veil of pain, it sees the light,
A phoenix rising, blazing through the night.
Each scar a tale of lessons learned,
Each flame a beacon, brightly burned,
In the crucible where hope returned,
A phoenix rises, undeterred.
Through the ashes of what once was,
Through the tears, through the loss,
Through the silence, through the pause,
A phoenix rises, bound by no laws.
In the labyrinth of despair and dread,
In the depths where dreams have fled,
In the silence where hope has bled,
A phoenix rises, its wings outspread.
For in the heart of every trial,
In the midst of every mile,

In the face of every trial,
A phoenix rises with a smile.
So let it rise, let it soar,
Let its song ring evermore,
For in its flames, we find the core,
Of strength and courage, evermore.
In the heart of the deepest night,
Where shadows dance and fears take flight,
A phoenix rises, burning bright,
A symbol of hope, in endless flight.

Resilience

Resilience, a whispered hymn in the heart's silent depths,
A dance with shadows, a symphony of strength.
In the crucible of trials, it finds its birth,
A phoenix rising from the ashes of despair.
It thrives in the echoes of shattered dreams,
In the quiet spaces where hope flickers and gleams.
With every tear shed, with every wound bared,
Resilience stands tall, unbroken, unscarred.
It's the steady rhythm of a beating heart,
A beacon of light in the darkest of parts.
In the face of adversity, it holds its ground,
A fortress of courage, profound and profound.
Through storms that rage and winds that wail,
Resilience endures, it will never fail.
For within its embrace lies the power to soar,
To rise above challenges, to triumph and more.
In the tapestry of life, it weaves its thread,
A testament to the spirit, to the paths we tread.
So let us embrace it, this force unyielding and true,
For in resilience, we find the strength to renew.
With every setback, with every fall,
Resilience whispers, "You can conquer it all."
So let it echo within, let it guide the way,
For in the journey of resilience, we find our brightest day.

The Garden of Self-Discovery

In the garden of self-discovery, where secrets softly lie,
Beneath the shade of ancient trees, 'neath the vast and endless sky,
There blooms a wondrous tapestry, in colors bright and bold,
Each petal tells a story, each leaf a tale untold.
Here, amidst the whispers of the breeze, and the songs of hidden streams,
The soul embarks on a journey, guided by its dreams.
Paths of uncertainty intertwine, through labyrinthine maze,
Yet every turn reveals anew, the sun's embracing blaze.
In this garden of self-discovery, where shadows dance and play,
The mirror of reflection shows the truth in gentle sway.
Acceptance is the fertile soil, where seeds of change take root,
And through the tender care of love, each bud begins to shoot.
Amidst the thorns of doubt and fear, resilience finds its bloom,
For in the face of adversity, the spirit learns to groom.
Through seasons of adversity, and storms that fiercely rage,
The garden of self-discovery finds solace on each page.
In every bloom, a lesson learned, in every leaf, a prayer,
In every thorn, a strength revealed, in every breath, a dare.
For in the garden of self-discovery, where mysteries softly sing,
The heart finds its true compass, beneath the sheltering wing.
So let us wander hand in hand, through pathways wild and free,
And in the garden of self-discovery, may we forever be,
For in the beauty of this journey, in the depths of its embrace,
We find the essence of our truth, our refuge, and our grace.

A New Dawn

In the quiet hush of night's embrace,
Where shadows dance and dreams take flight,
There lies a promise, a whispered grace,
A beacon glowing in the depths of night.
Through veils of darkness, stars alight,
A tapestry of hope, a shimmering sight,
Guiding weary souls through the unknown,
Toward the threshold where dreams are sown.
With each passing hour, the darkness wanes,
As dawn's tender fingers brush the sky,
A symphony of colors, a gentle refrain,
As night surrenders, bidding goodbye.
In the heart of dawn, a new beginning,
A canvas blank, awaiting its story,
Where echoes of yesterday are softly spinning,
And the promise of tomorrow shines in glory.
With the rising sun, a chorus sings,
A melody of hope, of endless possibility,
In the gentle breeze, hope takes wings,
And whispers of grace paint the tapestry.
For in each dawn, a world reborn,
A chance to mend, to heal, to grow,
To embrace the light that graces the morn,
And let the seeds of hope overflow.
So let us greet the dawn with open arms,
And cast aside the shadows of the night,
For in the birth of day, amidst its charms,
Lies the promise of a new dawn's light.

Mosaic of Healing

In the quiet corners of the heart's abode,
Where shadows linger, where scars have flowed,
There lies a mosaic, shattered, incomplete,
A kaleidoscope of memories, bittersweet.
Each fragment tells a story, etched in pain,
A symphony of struggles, a relentless rain,
Yet within the fractures, a whispering plea,
For healing to unravel, for wounds to set free.
Piece by piece, the fragments find their place,
A dance of colors, a delicate embrace,
For in the art of healing, there's a gentle grace,
A mosaic of resilience, a sacred space.
Through cracks and crevices, the light does seep,
Illuminating paths where sorrows sleep,
And as the mosaic takes its final form,
A tapestry of triumph, amidst the storm.
The brokenness, once scattered, now finds rest,
As healing's hand caresses, soft and blessed,
And in the mosaic's beauty, there's a tale untold,
Of strength and courage, of hearts grown bold.
So let us honor the mosaic of healing's art,
Embracing scars as symbols, of a resilient heart,
For in the fragments, lies a truth profound,
That from brokenness, beauty can be found.

In the Arms of Time

In the arms of time, where shadows fade,
And whispers of sorrow find solace in shade,
There lies a realm where healing's begun,
A sanctuary bathed in the light of the sun.
Through the corridors of memory, we roam,
Tracing the echoes of our hearts, our home,
In the stillness of moments, both tender and kind,
Lies the promise of solace, the peace we find.
Each tick of the clock, a gentle caress,
Softening the edges of pain's harshness,
For time is a river, flowing with grace,
Carrying fragments of sorrow to a distant place.
In the arms of time, wounds find their balm,
As the universe weaves its soothing psalm,
With each passing hour, a new chapter unfurls,
And the petals of hope, they softly swirl.
Though scars may linger, etched in the skin,
In the arms of time, new stories begin,
For in the tapestry of life, with its rhythm and rhyme,
We find sanctuary, we find healing, in the arms of time.

Echoes of Joy

In the quiet depths of the night, they sway,
Echoes of joy in the moon's soft array,
Whispers of laughter from days gone by,
In the hush of shadows, they gently lie.
They linger in the corners of my mind,
Fragments of moments, so gentle, so kind,
Memories wrapped in a golden hue,
In the tapestry of time, they renew.
In the quiet dawn of a brand-new day,
Echoes of joy, like a song, they sway,
Through the rustling leaves and the morning mist,
In the dance of light, they softly exist.
They sparkle in the laughter of a child,
In the warmth of embraces, tender and mild,
In the kindness shared, in the love that's true,
Echoes of joy, in the world anew.
They ripple through the rivers, swift and clear,
In the colors of sunset, drawing near,
In the embrace of nature's gentle embrace,
Echoes of joy, in every trace.
Though shadows may fall, and darkness may creep,
Echoes of joy, in my heart, they keep,
Guiding me forward, through valleys and peaks,
In the silence of hope, they softly speak.
So let them dance, in the depths of the night,
Echoes of joy, in the soft moonlight,
For in their whisper, I find my way,
To embrace the beauty of each new day.

The Tapestry of Hope

In the quiet corners of the heart's embrace,
    Where shadows dance in the light's soft grace,
    There lies a tapestry, woven with care,
    Threads of hope, delicate and rare.
    In the loom of life, where dreams take flight,
    Where darkness fades and gives way to light,
    Each strand tells a story, woven with love,
    A testament to the strength thereof.
    In the warp and weft of trials endured,
    In the silent prayers, in the songs obscured,
    Threads of courage, bold and bright,
    Interlace with threads of darkest night.
    Through the valleys of despair's domain,
    Through the echoes of sorrow's refrain,
    Hope's gentle touch, a guiding thread,
    Leading us where the soul is fed.
    In the tapestry of hope, colors blend,
    Shades of joy with sorrows mend,
    For every tear, a starry gleam,
    In every doubt, a hopeful dream.
    With every stitch, with every seam,
    The tapestry of hope begins to gleam,
    A mosaic of moments, stitched with care,
    A testament to the strength we bear.
    So let us weave with hands and heart,
    A tapestry of hope, a work of art,
    For in its threads, we find our way,
    Through darkest night, to brightest day.

Ripples of Positivity

In the quiet depths where shadows wane,
Beneath the surface, a gentle refrain,
Where troubles ebb and worries fade,
Ripples of positivity cascade.
From a single pebble, cast with care,
Echoes of hope dance in the air,
A simple act, a heartfelt deed,
Sends vibrations outward, planting the seed.
In the heart of darkness, a glimmer bright,
A beacon of warmth in the darkest night,
A smile shared, a hand outstretched,
Ripples of positivity effortlessly etched.
They travel far, these ripples wide,
Touching souls, no distance to hide,
Invisible threads of light they weave,
A tapestry of kindness, hearts believe.
With each embrace, with every sigh,
Ripples of positivity amplify,
A chorus of love, a symphony grand,
Uniting hearts across the land.
So let us be the pebble, let us be the source,
Spreading love, charting our course,
For in this world, where shadows loom,
Ripples of positivity light up the gloom.

Healing Waters

Beneath the moon's soft, silver glow,
Where shadows dance and breezes blow,
There lies a stream, a whispered tale,
Of healing waters that never fail.
In the hush of night, it softly sings,
A melody of profound springs,
With liquid notes that gently rise,
A balm for souls, a sweet surprise.
The stream, a mirror, reflects the sky,
Where troubles wane and sorrows fly,
Its ripples carry a healing grace,
Caressing hearts in a warm embrace.
Step into the waters, calm and deep,
Let currents of solace gently sweep,
Through tangled thoughts and weary bones,
Where healing waters have softly known.
Each droplet holds a whispered story,
Of strength reclaimed, of inner glory,
As liquid fingers weave a spell,
Beneath the moon, where secrets swell.
Feel the coolness on your skin,
A tender touch that heals within,
Washing away the stains of yore,
Leaving you lighter, cleansed, and more.
As time flows by, a gentle stream,
Healing waters, a tranquil dream,
Embrace the journey, let it flow,
In this sacred stream, let healing grow.

Blossoming

In the garden of the soul, where shadows dwell,
    Amidst the soil of struggles, a tale to tell,
    There lies a seed, dormant, waiting, unseen,
    Yearning to break free, where light has never been.
    Through the cracks of doubt, it sends its tender shoot,
    Pushing past the layers of darkness, taking root.
    In the quiet depths of the earth, it finds its way,
    Seeking the warmth of hope's gentle ray.
    With patient grace, it unfurls its delicate form,
    A silent anthem to resilience, weathering the storm.
    Each petal unfurling, a testament to the fight,
    Against the winds of despair, embracing the light.
    Through days of rain and nights of bitter frost,
    It holds steadfast, never counting the cost.
    For within its heart, a secret it keeps,
    The promise of beauty, even when the world weeps.
    With each passing dawn, it reaches for the sky,
    A symphony of color, a soul's sweet lullaby.
    In the garden of the soul, where shadows once held sway,
    A blossom blooms bravely, lighting the way.
    So let us learn from this flower, small yet bold,
    That even in darkness, beauty can unfold.
    For within each of us lies the power to rise,
    And blossom, despite the storms that may arise.

The Light Within

In the caverns of the soul, where shadows dance,
There lies a flame, a glimmer, a chance.
Amidst the darkness, where fears reside,
There burns a beacon, a light to guide.
In the depths of despair, where echoes cry,
There shines a spark, refusing to die.
Beneath the weight of sorrow's heavy shroud,
There gleams a glow, defiant and proud.
Through the maze of doubt, where whispers stray,
There flickers a flame, a hope to stay.
In the silence of the night, where dreams take flight,
There glows a warmth, a gentle, guiding light.
In the tumult of storms, where chaos reigns,
There beams a beacon, breaking through chains.
Against the backdrop of despair's dark hue,
There radiates a glow, steadfast and true.
For within the heart, where shadows fall,
There dwells a light, the brightest of all.
A flame of courage, burning bright and clear,
A beacon of hope, dispelling every fear.
So let it shine, this light within,
A ray of hope, where new days begin.
In every soul, let it ignite and soar,
The light within us, forevermore.

Sowing Seeds of Hope

In the quiet of the dawn's embrace,
Where shadows dance with morning grace,
I sow the seeds of hope in earth's embrace,
In the fertile soil, I find my place.
With gentle hands and tender care,
I plant the dreams that linger there,
Each seed a promise, a whispered prayer,
For growth, for strength, for life to bear.
Through sunlit days and gentle rain,
I watch the seeds begin to gain,
Their roots unfurl, their stems attain,
A testament to hope's refrain.
In darkest nights when shadows loom,
And doubts within my heart find room,
I turn to where the seedlings bloom,
And find in them the light's perfume.
For hope, it grows in quiet hours,
Amongst the petals, 'mongst the flowers,
In tender shoots and budding towers,
It thrives, it blooms, it empowers.
So let us sow the seeds of hope,
In valleys deep, on mountain slope,
For in our hands, we hold the scope,
To cultivate a world of trope.
And as we tend with love and care,
The seeds of hope, so pure and rare,
We find that life is ever fair,
When hope's bright flame, we choose to bear.

Section 4: Self-Care Rituals

Section 4 of "Whispers of the Soul: A Poetry Anthology on Mental Health and Well-being" delves into the intimate realm of self-care rituals, with Ismael S Rodriguez Jr's evocative poetry taking center stage. Through his verses, Ismael tenderly navigates the reader through the intricacies of self-nurturing practices, illuminating the profound significance of attending to one's own well-being amidst life's tumultuous waves. His poems resonate with the quiet strength found in moments of solitude, where the act of self-care becomes a sacred ritual, a sanctuary for the soul. Ismael's verses delicately unravel the layers of self-love and compassion, inviting readers to embrace the transformative power of simple gestures, whether it be the gentle caress of a morning breeze or the soothing warmth of a cup of tea. His words serve as a gentle reminder that amidst the chaos of existence, there exists solace in the tender embrace of self-care, nurturing the spirit and replenishing the essence of being.

Within Ismael's poetry, self-care transcends mere routine; it becomes a testament to resilience and an affirmation of self-worth. Through his introspective verses, Ismael paints a portrait of self-discovery, where the act of caring for oneself becomes an act of self-empowerment. In his poetry, self-care is not relegated to grand gestures but rather found in the quiet moments of reflection, in the tender embrace of self-compassion. Ismael's words resonate with authenticity, offering solace to those navigating the labyrinth of mental health struggles. With each stanza, he invites readers to embark on a journey of self-healing, where the nurturing of one's inner landscape becomes an act of profound self-love. In Ismael's poetry, self-care emerges as a beacon of light amidst the darkness, guiding the way towards wholeness and well-being.

Dawn's Reflection

In the hush before the sun's ascent,
Where dawn's whispers softly blend,
I find a space, serene and wide,
To let the world, and worries, slide.
Beneath the veil of morning's light,
In quiet corners of the night,
I sit in silence, calm and free,
Embracing what the day will be.
With eyes closed tight, I softly breathe,
Inhaling peace, exhaling ease,
Each breath a gentle, rhythmic flow,
Guiding me where I need to go.
In the stillness, thoughts arise,
Like clouds adrift in azure skies,
But I, the watcher, let them pass,
Like leaves that flutter in the grass.
I feel the earth beneath my feet,
The steady pulse of life's heartbeat,
And in this moment, here and now,
I find the strength to disavow
The fears that lingered through the night,
The doubts that clouded morning light,
For in this sacred space I've found,
A tranquil calm, profound, unbound.
As sunlight spills across the land,
I rise refreshed, with purpose grand,
For in the silence of the morn,
A new beginning is reborn.
So let the world in chaos spin,
For in this stillness, deep within,

I find the peace I seek to claim,
In morning's gentle, whispered refrain.

Nature's Healing Touch

In the heart of the forest, where shadows dance,
Nature's healing touch, a timeless trance.
Beneath the canopy, where sunlight peeks,
A sacred solace, where weary souls seek.
Through whispers of leaves, a melody flows,
Each rustle and murmur, a story it knows.
In the arms of the oak, worries unfurl,
As nature's embrace begins to swirl.
The babbling brook, a soothing song,
Carries away the burdens, all day long.
Its gentle rhythm, a lullaby sweet,
Guiding the weary to rest their feet.
On the horizon, where the sky meets earth,
Colors ablaze, a celestial birth.
The sunset's glow, a painting divine,
Casting away darkness, the soul to align.
In fields of wildflowers, dreams take flight,
Underneath the vast expanse of starry night.
Nature's healing touch, a balm for the soul,
In her embrace, we find ourselves whole.
So let us wander, where the wild things grow,
In nature's cathedral, where spirits flow.
For in her presence, we find our worth,
Nature's healing touch upon the earth.

Savoring Life

In kitchens where the sunlight streams,
The alchemy of life convenes,
Where pots and pans, and spices gleam,
And every meal is made to dream.
In every slice of vibrant green,
In every fruit, in every bean,
Lies the essence of a world unseen,
A dance of flavors, rich and keen.
For in the kitchen's sacred space,
We find a haven, a gentle place,
Where nourishment is not just taste,
But echoes of a deeper grace.
In every chop, in every stir,
We find communion, peace, and blur,
Where time stands still, and thoughts defer,
To the beauty of the cook's allure.
For food is more than sustenance,
It's poetry, its circumstance,
A symphony of sustenance,
A dance of flavor, form, and chance.
So let us gather 'round the table,
With hearts ablaze, and spirits able,
To savor every taste, every fable,
And find in food, our souls' revival.
For in the art of nourishment,
We find the essence of content,
A reminder of life's sweet ascent,
And all the blessings it has sent.

Morning's Golden Brew

In the quiet dawn's embrace, I rise,
    To greet the morn with sleepy eyes,
    A symphony of dawn birds' song,
    Welcoming the day, serene and long.
    Amidst the stillness, I find my way,
    To where the morning's promise lay,
    The kitchen, a sanctuary of peace,
    Where brewing magic shall never cease.
    With gentle hands, I fill the pot,
    With water clear, and never fraught,
    A measure of beans, dark and bold,
    Their fragrance, a tale yet untold.
    The grinder hums its ancient tune,
    As beans transform, under the moon,
    Into granules of liquid gold,
    A story waiting to unfold.
    The kettle sings its gentle song,
    As water dances, swift and strong,
    A union forged in morning's light,
    To bring forth joy, dispel the night.
    The aroma fills the silent air,
    A whispered promise, beyond compare,
    Of warmth and comfort, solace found,
    In every cup, in every sound.
    The steam ascends, a gentle wisp,
    A tender kiss, upon my lips,
    As cup meets saucer, hand meets brew,
    In this moment, I find my due.
    Each sip, a journey, rich and deep,
    A tapestry of flavors, secrets to keep,

From earthy notes to hints of spice,
Each sip, a moment, a paradise.
In the quiet cadence of the morn,
I find my solace, my spirit reborn,
In every drop, a world untold,
In every sip, a tale unfold.
For in this ritual, simple and true,
Lies the essence of morning's dew,
A brew of serenity, a cup of grace,
In the embrace of morning's embrace.

Elixir of Dawn: Dancing with the Sunrise

In the golden embrace of the breaking dawn,
    Where whispers of night bid their last adieu,
    There, beneath the waking sky, we're drawn,
    To dance with the sunrise, to start anew.
    In the stillness of morning's tender grace,
    A rhythm stirs, a melody takes flight,
    As shadows flee, and darkness yields its place,
    We spin and twirl, surrendering to light.
    With bare feet kissing the earth's dew-kissed skin,
    We move in harmony, a sacred trance,
    In every sway, a tale of hope begins,
    In every leap, a moment to enhance.
    The breeze becomes our partner, light and free,
    We waltz through fields where dreams and daisies grow,
    Each pirouette a symphony to see,
    Each step is a promise, each movement aglow.
    With arms outstretched, we reach for the sun's embrace,
    Its warm caress, a balm for weary souls,
    In every turn, we find a sacred space,
    Where broken hearts find healing, hearts are made whole.
    For in the dance, we find our truest voice,
    A language spoken by the heart's desire,
    In every motion, we rejoice,
    In every sway, we fan the flames of fire.
    With every beat, our spirits intertwine,
    In sync with nature's ancient, cosmic song,
    As day unfolds, we let our souls align,
    With every step, we feel where we belong.
    Oh, dancing with the sunrise, what a sight,
    To feel the earth beneath us, firm and true,

To dance away the shadows of the night,
And greet the morning with a heart anew.
For in the dance, we find our sanctuary,
A sacred temple, where our souls take flight,
Where movement is our prayer, our revelry,
And dawn becomes the canvas of our light.
So let us dance, my dear, with all our might,
Beneath the painted skies of dawn's embrace,
And greet the morning with unbridled delight,
As we dance with the sunrise, in this sacred space.

In the Garden of Reflection

In the Garden of Reflection, where shadows softly fall,
Each petal holds a story, each leaf a whispered call.
Beneath the azure sky, where time serenely flows,
The garden blooms with memories, where solace gently grows.
Here, amidst the fragrant blooms, a symphony of hues,
I tend to my inner garden, where whispers softly muse.
For just as flowers need their sun, and earth its gentle rain,
So too, the soul seeks nourishment, to ease away the pain.
Each blossom tells a tale of joy, of laughter in the sun,
But also, of the storms endured, of battles fought and won.
For every bloom that fades away, another takes its place,
A testament to resilience, a journey filled with grace.
I wander through the winding paths, where secrets gently hide,
And find a sanctuary of peace, where troubled thoughts subside.
The rustle of the leaves, the dance of dappled light,
It speaks to me of healing, of embracing the night.
In the Garden of Reflection, where silence finds its voice,
I learn the art of letting go, of making my own choice.
For just as roses need their thorns, and roots must dig down deep,
So too, the soul must find its strength, its promise it must keep.
I water tender shoots of hope, and prune away the doubt,
I cultivate the seeds of love and let forgiveness sprout.
For in this sacred space of mine, where dreams and shadows blend,
I find the courage to begin again, to journey to the end.
So let the roses bloom and fade, let the seasons turn and change,
For in the Garden of Reflection, nothing stays the same.
But through the ebb and flow of life, through every rise and fall,
I'll tend to my inner garden and find peace within it all.

Lunar Lullabies

Beneath the canopy of midnight's embrace,
    Where the silvered orb casts its gentle grace,
    There lies a sanctuary, tranquil and deep,
    Where souls find solace, and troubled hearts sleep.
    Amidst the whispers of the night's soft sigh,
    Beneath the luminous, velvet sky,
    A solitary figure sits in quiet repose,
    In the hush of twilight, where the tranquil river flows.
    Meditation's gentle rhythm takes its hold,
    As the mind, like a river, begins to unfold,
    A journey inward, to the depths of the soul,
    Where the secrets of the universe gently stroll.
    Bathed in the ethereal glow of the moon,
    In this sacred space, where silence croons,
    The seeker finds refuge from the noise of the day,
    In the tranquil embrace of the lunar ballet.
    Each breath becomes a melody, soft and slow,
    In the moonlit garden where dreams grow,
    With each exhale, worries gently fade,
    In the cradle of night, beneath the silver cascade.
    The rustle of leaves, a gentle caress,
    As the night's sweet whispers bring blessedness,
    The mind's chatter softens, fades away,
    In the tender embrace of the lunar ballet.
    Stars above twinkle, a celestial choir,
    In the canvas of night, hearts conspire,
    To dance in the stillness, to bathe in the light,
    Of the moon's gentle kiss, in the soft velvet night.
    In this sacred communion, time stands still,
    As the soul finds peace, in the quiet, the still,

In the moonlit meditation, where spirits unite,
In the embrace of the moon, in the embrace of the night.
And when the dawn breaks, with its golden hue,
And the night's gentle whispers bid adieu,
The seeker rises, with a heart at ease,
In the gentle glow of the moon, in the morning breeze.
For in the sanctuary of the moonlit night,
Where the soul takes flight, in the soft moonlight,
There lies the essence of tranquility,
In the moonlit meditation, in the soul's serenity.

Pages of Solitude

In the quiet corners of my room,
Where shadows dance and whispers loom,
I find my haven, my sacred space,
Amidst the silence, I embrace.
Pages of Solitude, my dear friend,
In your bindings, my heart finds mend.
With each turn, a world anew,
A refuge from the world I knew.
In the hush of evening's embrace,
I trace the lines upon your face.
Words like gentle raindrops fall,
Upon the canvas of my soul.
Through forests deep and oceans wide,
I wander with you by my side.
In tales of love and tales of woe,
I find the solace that I know.
With every character I meet,
I find reflections bittersweet.
In their trials, I see my own,
In their triumphs, seeds are sown.
In the dance of ink upon the page,
I find my solace, my refuge, my stage.
Each sentence a symphony, each paragraph a rhyme,
Guiding me through the labyrinth of time.
Oh, Pages of Solitude, how you understand,
The longing in my heart, the dreams that expand.
In your bound embrace, I find release,
From the cacophony, from the world's ceaseless peace.
As the hours wane and the stars alight,
I bid farewell to the world's harsh light.

For in your company, I find my truth,
In the quiet sanctuary of my youth.
So let the world spin, let the chaos reign,
For here in your arms, I remain.
With every page, a sanctuary found,
In the Pages of Solitude, my heart is bound.

Enchantment of the Woods

In whispers of leaves,
Nature's symphony echoes,
Soul finds solace here.
Among towering pines,
Ancient guardians stand tall,
Embrace me, forest.
Soft moss carpets ground,
Cool earth beneath my footsteps,
Nature's tender touch.
Sunlight filters through,
Golden threads of warmth and light,
Blessings from above.
Birdsong fills the air,
Melodies of life's dance,
Harmony surrounds.
Gentle stream meanders,
Crystal waters sing softly,
Flowing through the woods.
Fragrant blossoms bloom,
Perfume of wildflowers sweet,
Scent of pure delight.
Butterflies alight,
Dance in midsummer's embrace,
Joyful in their flight.
Forest whispers secrets,
Whispers of ancient wisdom,
Echoes of the past.
Time slows in the woods,
Nature's rhythm guides my soul,
Peaceful, tranquil heart.

In forest's embrace,
I find healing, find myself,
Lost and found in woods.
Shinrin-yoku, balm,
Nature's remedy for woes,
Healing in the woods.
Let the forest heal,
Breathe in the sacred essence,
Find peace in its arms.
Enchantment of woods,
A sanctuary for the soul,
In nature, we thrive.
May the forest's grace,
Soothe the weary, troubled heart,
And bring inner peace.
In the woods, we find,
A sanctuary of calm,
Nature's gentle embrace.

Canvas of Colors: A Symphony of Self-Care

In the quiet sanctuary of the artist's room,
Where sunlight dances and shadows bloom,
There lies a canvas, blank and bare,
Awaiting the touch of colors rare.
With brush in hand, the artist stands,
Lost in the world of his own commands,
Each stroke a whisper, each hue a song,
In this sacred space where he belongs.
With every dab, a piece of soul,
Spills onto the canvas, making it whole,
Each color speaks of joy and pain,
Of dreams pursued, and fears slain.
In swirls of blue, the sky takes flight,
A realm of endless, boundless light,
Where dreams are born and hopes ascend,
In the artist's world, there is no end.
With shades of green, the earth awakes,
In forests deep, and meadows wide,
Where life begins, and stories unfold,
In every leaf, a tale untold.
In fiery reds, the passion burns,
A symphony of desire, the heart yearns,
For love embraced, and dreams pursued,
In the canvas of colors, all is renewed.
With gentle strokes, the artist weaves,
A tapestry of memories, of hopes, and dreams,
Each line a journey, each color a sigh,
In the canvas of colors, he finds his why.

And when the painting is finally done,
And the colors fade with the setting sun,
The artist smiles, his heart at ease,
For in the canvas of colors, he finds his peace.
For in the act of creation, he finds release,
From the burdens of the world, he finds his ease,
In the canvas of colors, he finds his truth,
A testament to the beauty of youth.
So let the colors dance, let the brushes play,
In the canvas of colors, let us find our way,
To a world of beauty, where dreams take flight,
In the canvas of colors, let there be light.

Aromatherapy Dreams

In the tranquil realm where dreams take flight,
    Amidst the hush of the velvety night,
    There lies a path of fragrant streams,
    An odyssey of soothing, sweet dreams.
    Aromatherapy whispers softly, its tale,
    In fragrant notes that gently sail,
    Through the corridors of the mind's embrace,
    A journey of serenity, a tranquil space.
    Inhale the essence of lavender's bloom,
    As moonbeams dance in a tranquil room,
    Where candles flicker, casting their glow,
    Upon the tapestry of shadows below.
    The air is laced with jasmine's grace,
    A symphony of scents, a sacred place,
    Where worries dissolve in the tranquil mist,
    And the soul finds solace, gently kissed.
    Beneath the canopy of stars above,
    The senses awaken to nature's love,
    As eucalyptus whispers secrets untold,
    In the tranquil night, so calm and bold.
    Breathe in the essence of chamomile's sigh,
    As the world outside begins to lie,
    In peaceful slumber, beneath the moon's soft gleam,
    In the sanctuary of an aromatherapy dream.
    Each scent a story, each aroma a song,
    That carries the weary heart along,
    To distant shores of tranquility,
    Where the spirit finds its serenity.
    So let the fragrance guide you, softly, dear,
    To a place where worries disappear,

And let the gentle whispers of the night,
Fill your soul with tranquility's light.
For in the realm where dreams take flight,
Amidst the hush of the velvety night,
There lies a path of fragrant streams,
An odyssey of soothing, sweet dreams.

In the Flow: Yoga Pose Poetry

In the gentle hush of morning light,
    Where dawn's embrace meets the breaking night,
    There lies a practice, serene and deep,
    Where body and soul in harmony meet.
    In mountain's grace, we find our start,
    Rooted firm, yet open heart,
    With arms stretched high, like branches sway,
    We greet the sun, this brand-new day.
    Warrior's stance, both fierce and bold,
    In strength we stand, our stories told,
    With gaze fixed forward, spirits rise,
    In the dance of breath, the soul's own cries.
    Downward dog, a humble bow,
    Inverted arch, we find it now,
    A moment's pause, a quiet prayer,
    To surrender, release, and tender care.
    Child's pose, a sweet retreat,
    In the cradle of earth, we find our seat,
    With forehead kissed by mother's grace,
    We find solace in this sacred space.
    Lotus blooms, serene and still,
    In tranquil waters, hearts fulfill,
    With petals open, minds align,
    In the silence, the divine's design.
    Corpse pose, the final rest,
    In stillness, we are truly blessed,
    With breath as guide, we journey deep,
    To the place where dreams and whispers meet.
    In each pose, a story told,
    Of strength, surrender, and truths behold,

For in the flow of yoga's grace,
We find our center, our sacred place.
So let us breathe, and let us be,
In the dance of life, wild and free,
For in the poetry of yoga's art,
We find the peace that fills the heart.

Stargazing Reverie

Beneath the cosmic quilt, a tapestry divine,
The ink-black canvas, where stars brightly shine.
Eyes lifted heavenward, souls take flight,
In the velvet night, bathed in lunar light.

I. Prelude to the Cosmos

Breathe in the nocturnal air, crisp and cool,
As the celestial ballet begins its ethereal rule.
Galaxies twirl, a cosmic ballet unseen,
In this astral theater, where dreams convene.

II. Orion's Elegance

Orion strides across the obsidian stage,
A celestial hunter, fierce and sage.
His belt, a beacon in the cosmic sea,
Guiding seekers to the wonders to be.

III. Whispers of the Milky Way

Silver strands of the Milky Way's braid,
Stories of the cosmos silently laid.
Each star, a verse in the universal song,
Whispers of eternity where we belong.

IV. The Dance of Jupiter and Mars

Gaze upon the planets, distant and bright,
Jupiter's majesty, Mars' warrior light.
They waltz in celestial grandeur,
A cosmic dance, a celestial fervor.

V. Luna's Lullaby

The moon, a guardian, in wax and wane,
A luminous pearl in the night's terrain.
Her craters and seas, a lunar map,
Guiding the dreamers in their midnight nap.

VI. Andromeda's Tapestry
Far beyond the reach of mortal sight,
Andromeda weaves her cosmic kite.
A galaxy, a tapestry in silk,
A quilt of stars, a cosmic milk.
VII. A Telescope's Gaze
Yet, a telescope unveils more,
Peeling back the cosmic lore.
Galactic wonders, nebulae aglow,
In this celestial theater's grand show.
VIII. Celestial Reflections
Stars, distant suns in cosmic seas,
Each story whispered on cosmic breeze.
The vastness above, a canvas unfurled,
A reflection of the infinitesimal world.

IX. Earth's Insignificance
In the quiet of this celestial trance,
Life's tribulations begin to dance.
For in the cosmos' grand design,
Our worries dwindle, our troubles resign.
X. The Astral Connection
Bathed in starlight, a connection profound,
Astronomy's magic, an eternal playground.
In the vastness, life's struggles seem small,
A cosmic perspective, embracing all.
XI Journey Homeward
As the night bids adieu, the stars softly fade,
The universe whispers, a serenade.
Returning to Earth, a transformed gaze,

In the stardust of dreams, our spirit stays.

XII. Epilogue: Celestial Embrace
So, in the quiet of a stargazing reverie,
We find solace in the cosmic tapestry.
Embraced by the universe, troubles grow dim,
In the vast celestial sea, we learn to swim.

Digital Detox Ode

In the hushed embrace of silence, where echoes fade,
    There lies a sanctuary, where souls find aid.
    Amidst the static hum of our digital age,
    Lies wisdom in disconnecting, turning the page.
    Ode to the Digital Detox, a sacred quest,
    To unplug the wires, find peace, and rest.
    In the glow of screens, where time swiftly flies,
    Lies the need for stillness, beneath vast skies.
    Oh, how we're entwined in the web's woven threads,
    Lost in the chaos, where clarity sheds.
    But amidst the noise, there's a whispering call,
    To reclaim our essence, to stand, to fall.
    In the quietude of dawn's gentle rise,
    There's solace found under cerulean skies.
    No beeping alerts or notifications in sight,
    Just the gentle murmur of morning light.
    In forests deep, where nature's hymn sings,
    There's solace found beneath verdant wings.
    Away from pixels, where the heart can breathe,
    Amongst rustling leaves, we find reprieve.
    Let's wander afar from the digital shore,
    To realms where simplicity opens the door.
    Where conversations bloom without a screen's glare,
    And laughter dances in the open air.
    Digital Detox, oh, how sweet the sound,
    Of silence reigning, as distractions drown.
    In unplugged moments, our spirits revive,
    As we reconnect with the rhythms of life.
    No longer slaves to the digital stream,
    We awaken from the confines of a digital dream.

In the stillness, we find what truly matters,
In unplugging, we rediscover life's splendors.
So let us raise a hymn to the Digital Detox,
To reclaiming our time, our minds unboxed.
For in the silence, clarity is found,
In the unplugged moments, peace does abound.
Let's cherish the moments where screens fade away,
And embrace the gift of a slower, quieter day.
For in the silence, we find our way back home,
To the essence of being, where hearts freely roam.

Threads of Connection

In the tapestry of life, threads intertwine,
Binding hearts together, in a dance divine.
A symphony of souls, in harmony's embrace,
Weaving stories of love, hope, and grace.
In the laughter shared under the open sky,
In the tears shed when sorrows draw nigh,
In the quiet moments of understanding deep,
Connections bloom, like promises we keep.
Hands held tight, in moments of fear,
Voices raised, when joy draws near.
In the warmth of a smile, in a glance so kind,
True connections, in the heart, we find.
Through the ebb and flow of life's grand scheme,
We find solace in the connections we gleam.
In the embrace of friendship, pure and true,
We find the strength to see each journey through.
For in the heart of every soul we meet,
Lies the echo of our own heartbeat.
In the tapestry of life, woven strong and free,
We find our truest selves in the community.
So let us cherish each connection we hold dear,
For in these bonds, our spirits find cheer.
In the beauty of togetherness, we find our worth,
For it's in connecting with others, we find rebirth.

Embrace Within

In the quiet chambers of the heart's embrace,
Where shadows dance with light upon the face,
There lies a journey, winding and slow,
Where self-compassion and forgiveness grow.
Beneath the layers of doubt and pain,
A whisper lingers, softly to explain,
That to forgive is to release the chains,
And to embrace the self with gentle reins.
Let go of judgments, let go of fear,
For in the mirror, a friend is near,
Reflecting back the beauty that's within,
And all the flaws that make us human kin.
No need for perfection in this sacred space,
Just grace to stumble, to fall, to embrace,
The tender wounds that shape our souls anew,
And the strength to rise, forgiving through and through.
For in the garden of forgiveness, we find,
The seeds of love that blossom in the mind,
And in the depths of self-compassion's gaze,
We learn to cherish our imperfect ways.
So let us walk this path with open eyes,
And with each step, let empathy arise,
For in the journey of self-forgiveness true,
We find the love that heals and sees us through.

Section 5: Mind-Body Connection

In Section 5, titled "Mind-Body Connection," Ismael S Rodriguez Jr's poetry emerges as a profound exploration of the intricate relationship between mental and physical well-being. Through his verses, Ismael offers a lyrical examination of the symbiotic nature of the mind and body, weaving together themes of introspection, resilience, and the pursuit of holistic health. His poetry delicately navigates the interconnectedness of mental and physical states, illuminating the ways in which thoughts, emotions, and physical sensations intertwine to shape our overall well-being. Through vivid imagery and introspective narratives, Rodriguez invites readers to contemplate the profound impact of the mind-body connection on our daily lives and the journey towards inner harmony.

Within the confines of Section 5, Ismael's poetic voice stands out as a beacon of insight and introspection, guiding readers on a transformative exploration of self-awareness and holistic wellness. With each carefully crafted verse, Rodriguez delves into the depths of human experience, inviting readers to confront the complexities of their own mind-body connection. Through poignant reflections and evocative imagery, his poetry serves as a testament to the power of mindfulness, self-care, and the conscious cultivation of well-being. By intertwining themes of self-discovery and healing, Ismael's work resonates deeply, offering solace and inspiration to those navigating the intricate dance between mind and body in their pursuit of a balanced and fulfilling life.

Breath of Life

In the quiet depths where silence thrives,
    Where whispers dance and echoes strive,
    There lies a gift, so pure, so rife,
    The breath of life, the essence of strife.
    Inhale, exhale, a sacred dance,
    A rhythm of chance, a fleeting trance,
    In every rise, in every fall,
    Lies the secret to heed nature's call.
    O breath of life, serene and still,
    You guide us through the darkest chill,
    With every sigh, with every sigh,
    You teach us how to live, to fly.
    In moments vast, in moments small,
    You hold the key, you break the wall,
    Through tangled thoughts and fears untold,
    You lead us to a peace, behold.
    When storms rage and tempests roar,
    And chaos reigns forevermore,
    You are the calm amidst the storm,
    The anchor in our hearts, so warm.
    With gentle touch, you soothe the soul,
    You make us whole; you make us whole,
    Inhale, exhale, a sacred vow,
    To find our center, here and now.
    In the temple of the present hour,
    You grant us strength, you grant us power,
    To face the trials, to face the test,
    And find the peace within our chest.
    In breath we find the universe,
    Inhale the stars, exhale the curse,

For in the rhythm of our breath,
Lies the key to life, beyond all death.
So let us honor, let us cherish,
This sacred bond that will not perish,
For in the breath of life we find,
The power to heal, to grow, to shine.
Inhale, exhale, the cycle's song,
In every breath, we all belong,
To the eternal dance of being,
To the sacred gift we're all seeing.
O breath of life, we sing your praise,
In every moment, in every phase,
For you are the bridge, the sacred tie,
Between the mind, the body, the sky.
So let us breathe, let us be,
Inhale the truth, exhale the free,
For in the breath of life, we find,
The calm, the peace, the light divine.

Dance of Mind and Muscle

In the quiet space where thoughts take flight,
Where the mind meets the body's gentle might,
There lies a dance, both subtle and grand,
A union of spirit, a joining hand in hand.
In the rhythm of breath, in the beat of the heart,
Where the soul finds solace, where troubles depart,
There blooms a grace, serene and whole,
A harmony born from the depths of the soul.
In the stretch of the limbs, in the sway of the spine,
Where movement becomes a sacred shrine,
There flows a language, ancient and pure,
A dialogue whispered, intimate and sure.
With each graceful arc, with each steady stance,
The body speaks, in a silent dance,
And the mind, it listens, in tranquil repose,
As worries dissolve, and serenity grows.
In the stillness of yoga, in the freedom of dance,
There's a symphony played, a fleeting trance,
Where the burdens of life find their sweet release,
And the spirit finds nourishment, finding peace.
Oh, Dance of Mind and Muscle, gentle and free,
You unlock the gates to serenity,
In your embrace, we find our center, our core,
And in your rhythm, we find ourselves, evermore.

In the Stillness

In the stillness of the morning air,
    Where silence whispers secrets rare,
    I find a space untouched by time,
    A sanctuary for the soul to climb.
    With eyes closed, I seek the quietude,
    Where thoughts dissolve like misty dew,
    And in the hush, I gently tread,
    Upon the path where stillness led.
    No rush of day nor clamor's call,
    Disturbs the peace within these walls,
    For here, within this sacred space,
    I find a refuge, a silent grace.
    In the stillness, I find my breath,
    A steady rhythm, life's dance and depth,
    Each inhale a moment, pure and bright,
    Each exhale a release, a soft goodnight.
    In the depths of silence, I find my voice,
    A whispered prayer, a quiet rejoice,
    For here, within this sacred hush,
    I find the essence of life's gentle brush.
    In the stillness, time stands still,
    And every moment holds its fill,
    Of peace, of presence, of grace untold,
    In the stillness, I find my soul.
    So let me linger in this tranquil space,
    Where silence holds its gentle embrace,
    And in the stillness, let me find,
    The quietude that heals the mind.

The Language of Touch

In the quiet realm where whispers roam,
There lies a language, silent yet known,
It speaks in touches, soft and kind,
A gentle solace for hearts entwined.
In the language of touch, there is no sound,
Yet in its embrace, sweet solace is found,
It speaks of comfort, of love's warm glow,
In tender moments, its essence does flow.
With fingertips tracing paths unknown,
It tells of stories, untold, unshown,
In the brush of a hand, a world's embrace,
Healing wounds, offering grace.
In the tender graze of fingers light,
Lies the power to make all things right,
For in the dance of skin on skin,
Hearts find solace, begin to mend.
In the language of touch, there's no need for words,
For it speaks in whispers, softer than birds,
It tells of empathy, of shared delight,
In the language of touch, hearts take flight.
In the gentle stroke across a weary brow,
Lies the promise of a brighter now,
In the warmth of an embrace, troubles fade away,
As love's gentle touch leads the way.
In the language of touch, there's healing power,
In the embrace of a friend, in the darkest hour,
It speaks of hope, of strength within,
In the language of touch, we begin again.
With hands entwined, hearts beat as one,
In the language of touch, battles are won,

For in the simple act of reaching out,
Lies the courage to dispel doubt.
So let us speak in the language of touch,
In moments tender, in moments much,
For in the connection of skin to skin,
Lies the beauty of the human within.
In the language of touch, let love reside,
In the gentle caress, let hearts confide,
For in the silence of an embrace so tight,
Lies the language of touch, pure and bright.

Garden of the Soul

In the quiet recesses of the mind,
Lies a garden, lush and undefined.
Where thoughts and dreams intertwine,
In the tender embrace of the divine.
In this garden of the soul,
Seeds of hope and fears take their toll.
Where shadows dance in the moon's soft glow,
And whispers of the heart begin to flow.
Each flower, a thought, delicate and fair,
Blooms with the fragrance of a prayer.
Some vibrant, with colors bright,
Others, shrouded in the depths of night.
The sun, a beacon in the sky above,
Nurtures this garden with warmth and love.
Its rays, like gentle hands that tend,
To the tender shoots that ascend.
But there are weeds that twist and twine,
Threatening to choke this garden divine.
Doubt and worry, like thorns they grow,
Entwining, suffocating, in a relentless flow.
Yet amidst the chaos, there's a melody,
A song of hope that sets the spirit free.
For in this garden, there's magic untold,
Where dreams take flight, and stories unfold.
Tread softly, oh seeker of truth,
For the garden holds secrets of youth.
Its pathways winding, mysterious and deep,
Where the soul's secrets silently keep.
In the stillness of the early morn,
The garden whispers, a truth reborn.

That to tend this land, we must first seek,
The seeds of wisdom, the truths we speak.
With hands outstretched and hearts aglow,
We nurture this garden, let our spirits grow.
For in its depths, lies the essence of being whole,
In the sacred sanctuary, the Garden of the Soul.
So, tend it well, this garden fair,
With love and kindness, with tender care.
For in its blooms, we find our truth,
In the whispers of the soul, the eternal youth.
Let thoughts and emotions freely roam,
In this sanctuary we call home.
For in the garden, we find our peace,
Where the soul's sweet melodies never cease.
In the garden of the soul, we find our truth,
In its blossoms lies the fountain of youth.
So let us tend it with love and care,
For in its depths, we find solace rare.
In the garden of the soul, we find our way,
In its shadows and light, we learn to stay.
For in its beauty, lies the key,
To unlock the mysteries of eternity.
In the garden of the soul, we find our rest,
In its embrace, we are truly blessed.
For in its whispers, we hear our song,
In the garden of the soul, we belong.

Rhythm of Life

In the quiet hush of dawn's embrace,
Where morning light paints the sky's face,
There lies a rhythm, soft and true,
A whispering pulse that beats anew.
It echoes deep within our core,
A timeless dance, forevermore,
The rhythm of life, a sacred song,
In every heartbeat, we belong.
In sync with nature's gentle flow,
Our souls entwine, our spirits grow,
For in the rustle of the trees,
And in the hum of honeybees,
We find a symphony so grand,
A harmony that's hand in hand,
With every breath, with every sigh,
The rhythm of life draws nigh.
It speaks in whispers on the breeze,
And in the rustling of the leaves,
It pulses through the ocean's tide,
And in the stars that brightly glide.
With each sunrise, with each sunset,
In moments we cannot forget,
The rhythm of life beats strong and clear,
A constant presence, ever near.
So let us dance to nature's tune,
Beneath the glowing, silver moon,
And feel the pulse of earth's embrace,
As we become one with time and space.
For in the rhythm of life's sweet refrain,
We find our solace, we find our bane,

Yet through it all, we learn to thrive,
In harmony with all alive.

Healing Hands

In the quiet realm where words dissolve,
And shadows linger, deep and cold,
There lies a language, soft and pure,
A touch that speaks, forever sure.
In hands that reach with tender grace,
A healing balm, a sacred space,
Where pain finds solace, finds release,
And burdens ease, as whispers cease.
These hands, they carry tales untold,
Of wounds that ache, of stories bold,
They speak in silence, soft and kind,
A language of the heart, refined.
With fingertips that trace the scars,
They mend the broken, soothe the stars,
They hold the weight of weary souls,
And cradle dreams, making them whole.
In every gentle stroke they lend,
A symphony of hope transcends,
For touch, a bridge, a sacred art,
That binds the broken, mends the heart.
So let us honor healing hands,
In them, the power to understand,
That in the silence, love is found,
In touch, the sweetest, softest sound.

The Art of Listening

In silence, where echoes softly reside,
Amidst the whispers of the soul's stride,
Lies the art of listening, profound and deep,
Where the body's voice begins to speak.
Not with words, nor with spoken tongue,
But with sensations, soft and strong,
It whispers secrets, both gentle and wise,
In the language of heart's quiet sighs.
Listen closely to the rhythm's call,
The heartbeat's dance, the rise and fall,
Each pulse a story, each breath a tale,
Of the journey within, where truths prevail.
In the symphony of senses, let us find,
The melody of presence, pure and kind,
For in the stillness, where the whispers play,
Lies the path to understanding, come what may.

Whispers of the Wind

In the quiet hush of twilight's grace,
Where shadows linger and dreams embrace,
There dances the wind, with whispers so light,
Echoing thoughts in the depths of night.
Like the gentle breeze through branches weaved,
Thoughts meander, as leaves perceived,
Fluttering softly, in the mind's expanse,
In the silent dance of mindful trance.
Listen now, to the wind's soft song,
As it carries echoes, sweet and strong,
In its passage, let thoughts gently flow,
Like leaves on the breeze, to come and go.
For in the ebb and flow of the wind's gentle sway,
Lies the wisdom of letting thoughts drift away,
In the vastness of sky, and the depth of mind,
Find solace in letting go, and peace you'll find.

Somatic Symphony

In the quiet chambers of the soul's domain,
Where whispers of the body's wisdom reign,
There lies a symphony, serene and true,
A melody of senses, both old and new.
In every beat, a rhythm softly hums,
A dance of life, where every pulse becomes
A note in the grand score of being whole,
A symphony of body, heart, and soul.
The skin, a canvas touched by gentle breeze,
A whispering of leaves beneath tall trees,
Each sensation, a brushstroke on the air,
Painting portraits of joy, of love, of care.
The heart, a drum that echoes with each beat,
A steady rhythm, strong and ever sweet,
A cadence of emotions, raw and free,
Guiding us to who we're meant to be.
In every breath, a song of life is sung,
A melody that binds us, old and young,
A harmony that weaves through every vein,
A reminder of our shared earthly plane.
So let us listen to the somatic song,
And in its echoes, may we all belong,
For in the symphony of flesh and bone,
We find the truth that we are not alone.
Tune in, dear soul, to this celestial art,
And let the music heal the wounded heart,
For in the somatic symphony we find,
The essence of our being intertwined.

Dance of Endorphins

In the realm where spirits soar and muscles gleam,
Where the heart finds rhythm, and dreams take their stream,
There lies a sanctuary, vibrant and bright,
Where the dance of endorphins ignites the night.
In the temple of movement, where bodies align,
And the echoes of laughter sweetly entwine,
There, amidst the sweat and the beat of the drum,
Endorphins awaken, a symphony begun.
Feel the pulse of vitality, coursing through veins,
As the body rejoices, releasing its chains,
In the dance of endorphins, the soul takes flight,
Embracing the joy that comes with the night.
With every step, every leap, every bound,
The world spins around, in harmonious sound,
Muscles awaken, aching to play,
In the rhythm of motion, they find their own way.
Through the sweat and the strain, there's a song in the air,
As endorphins cascade, banishing care,
In the midst of the chaos, a calm settles in,
As the dance of endorphins begins to begin.
It's the rush of euphoria, the thrill of the chase,
In the dance of endorphins, there's no better place,
To feel the pulse of life, to embrace the unknown,
To dance to the rhythm of flesh and of bone.
In the beat of the music, in the sway of the hips,
There's a freedom that comes with each sway and each dip,
As the body surrenders to the joy of the night,
In the dance of endorphins, all worries take flight.
So let us dance, let us revel and play,
In the ecstasy found in the light of the day,

For in the dance of endorphins, we find our release,
And in the joy of movement, our souls find their peace.
In the dance of endorphins, we find our true worth,
In the rhythm of movement, we conquer the earth,
For in the embrace of the night, we find our own grace,
And in the dance of endorphins, we find our own place.

Dreams in Motion

In the hush of dawn's gentle glow,
Where dreams and reality intertwine,
There lies a tale of motion's flow,
A dance of spirit, a rhythm divine.
In the sinew's stretch and the muscle's flex,
Lies the heartbeat of dreams set free,
A symphony of motion, complex,
Where the mind finds solace, finds glee.
For in each stride upon the earth,
In every leap toward the sky,
Lies a journey of infinite worth,
Where dreams and motion learn to fly.
In the runner's rhythm, swift and fleet,
In the dancer's grace, light as air,
Lies a language both subtle and sweet,
A melody of dreams beyond compare.
With every step, with every turn,
The mind finds release, finds devotion,
In the fire that within does burn,
In the dreams that stir, in the ocean.
For motion is the canvas wide,
Where dreams paint strokes both bold and bright,
Where aspirations, with each stride,
Take flight into the depths of night.
In the marathoner's steady pace,
In the yogi's pose, serene and still,
Lies the echo of dreams' embrace,
The promise of dreams fulfilled.
With each heartbeat, with each breath,
Comes the stirring of aspirations deep,

In the symphony of life and death,
In the dreams that rise from sleep.
For dreams in motion find their power,
In the journey of the body's grace,
In the dawn's first light, in the midnight hour,
In the sacred dance, in the secret place.
So let us dance upon the breeze,
Let us run beneath the open sky,
For in motion's embrace, we find release,
And in dreams, we find wings to fly.
In the connection between body and mind,
In the pursuit of aspirations grand,
Lies the truth that we seek to find,
In dreams in motion, hand in hand.

Section 6: Seeking Support

In Section 6 of "Whispers of the Soul: A Poetry Anthology on Mental Health and Well-being," Ismael S Rodriguez Jr's poignant verses take center stage, offering profound insights into the significance of seeking support amidst mental health challenges. Through his evocative poetry, Ismael intricately weaves narratives of vulnerability and resilience, highlighting the transformative power of human connection in navigating turbulent emotional landscapes. With each verse, Ismael invites readers into the intimate realm of seeking solace and understanding, where the embrace of loved ones and the warmth of community become beacons of hope in the darkest of nights. His words resonate deeply, reminding us of the importance of reaching out, of breaking the silence, and of finding strength in the collective embrace of those who understand.

Ismael's poetry in this section not only sheds light on the struggles individuals face but also underscores the inherent strength found in seeking support. Through his verses, Ismael delicately explores the nuances of vulnerability and the healing that comes from sharing one's burdens with trusted companions. His poetry serves as a reminder that seeking support is not a sign of weakness but rather an act of courage, a step towards reclaiming one's sense of agency and well-being. Ismael's unique voice amplifies the anthology's overarching message, advocating for empathy, understanding, and the power of human connection in the journey towards mental health and well-being.

The Circle of Light

In the hush of night, where shadows dance,
    Amidst the echoes of a silent trance,
    There lies a circle, warm and bright,
    A beacon glowing through the darkest night.
It's born from hearts that seek to share,
To soothe the wounds, to show they care,
A gathering of souls, both near and far,
United by a guiding star.
In the circle's glow, whispers rise,
Each tale a tear, each voice a prize,
For in the sharing, burdens ease,
And hope ignites, a gentle breeze.
Here, amidst the tender embrace,
No judgment lurks, no masked face,
Just understanding, pure and true,
A sanctuary for me and you.
In the center, a flame burns bright,
A symbol of love, a guiding light,
It flickers with the stories told,
With laughter, tears, and dreams unfold.
From every corner, every shore,
The circle widens even more,
Embracing those who yearn to find
A refuge from the stormy grind.
In the circle of light, we find our kin,
A family forged from deep within,
With hands outstretched, we bridge the gap,
And walk together, hand in hand.
For in our unity, we rise,
Defeating darkness with our cries,

We are the circle, strong and bold,
A testament to love untold.
So let us gather, let us sing,
Let our voices soar on gentle wing,
For in this circle, we find our might,
Guided by the eternal light.

The Listening Ear

In the heart of twilight's gentle embrace,
Where shadows dance in silent grace,
There lies a tale of solace and cheer,
A timeless ode to the listening ear.
Amidst the chaos of the bustling day,
When troubles weigh and spirits sway,
There blooms a haven, calm and near,
In the whispering depths of the listening ear.
It's not just flesh, not just bone,
But a sanctuary where souls find home,
A vessel of empathy, warm and clear,
Where burdens lighten, where sorrows disappear.
In the hush of night, beneath the stars' soft gleam,
The listening ear, like a tranquil stream,
Waits patiently, without a trace of fear,
To catch the echoes of a soul sincere.
It hears the tales of joy and woe,
The highs, the lows, the ebb and flow,
With tenderness, it draws them near,
Each word, each sigh, it holds dear.
It cradles secrets, spoken in trust,
Embraces fears, releases the dust
Of doubts that linger, year after year,
In the comforting arms of the listening ear.
No judgment here, no harsh decree,
Just understanding, pure and free,
A silent witness, a friend so dear,
Guiding through the maze of doubt and fear.
Through laughter and tears, it stands steadfast,
A beacon of hope in the shadows cast,

An anchor in storms, a haven clear,
The unwavering grace of the listening ear.
For in the art of listening, hearts entwine,
In the silence, connections divine,
And though words may falter, the soul can steer,
Towards healing and light, with the listening ear.
So let us honor this gift so rare,
With gratitude, with utmost care,
For in the tapestry of life's grand sphere,
Nothing shines brighter than the listening ear.

Together We Stand

In the heart of the storm, where shadows loom,
And darkness threatens to consume,
We find our strength, we find our light,
In the bonds that hold, in the depths of night.
Hand in hand, we brave the gale,
Facing fears that would make hearts pale,
For in our unity, in our embrace,
We find the courage to stand in grace.
Through trials fierce and battles won,
In the rising of the morning sun,
We stand as one, no soul apart,
Bound by love, a beating heart.
In whispered words and knowing eyes,
In shared tears and heartfelt sighs,
We find our refuge, we find our might,
In the unity of our collective sight.
For when we stand, hand in hand,
No tempest can tear us from the land,
United souls, in strength arrayed,
Together we stand, undismayed.
Through every trial, through every test,
In the crucible of life, we find our best,
For in our togetherness, we understand,
That together we stand, hand in hand.

Bridges of Understanding

In the realm where hearts dare to meet,
Amidst the whispers of souls complete,
There lies a bridge, sturdy and true,
Forged from empathy, from me to you.
Its arches stretch across the divide,
Where shadows linger, where doubts reside,
But upon its span, a light does gleam,
A beacon of hope, a shared dream.
With each step taken, fears dissolve,
As we walk together, problems resolve,
For on this bridge, understanding reigns,
In every whisper, in every refrain.
We weave our stories, our sorrows, our joys,
Building connections, mending life's ploys,
Through the language of compassion, we speak,
In the silence, in the words we seek.
No chasm too wide, no barrier too tall,
For empathy knows no bounds at all,
And as we traverse this bridge of grace,
We find in each other a sacred place.
So let us journey, hand in hand,
Across this bridge, where souls expand,
For in the meeting of minds, we find,
The beauty of hearts, intertwined.
In the dance of understanding, we find release,
A sanctuary where conflicts cease,
And on this bridge, under skies so blue,
We discover the essence of me, of you.
Let us walk this path with hearts entwined,
Where empathy's light forever shines,

For in the embrace of understanding's glow,
We find the strength to heal, to grow.
Bridges of understanding, built with care,
A testament to the love we share,
May they stand eternal, in every land,
Guiding us forward, hand in hand.

The Comfort of Presence

In the silence, amid shadows deep,
Where sorrows linger and troubles sleep,
There lies a solace, a gentle grace,
In the tender embrace of a comforting face.
No words are needed, no tales to tell,
Just the presence, a soothing spell,
A quiet understanding, unspoken and clear,
A refuge of calm in the midst of fear.
In the darkest hours, when shadows loom,
And the heart is heavy, consumed by gloom,
There's a beacon of light, a guiding star,
In the gentle presence, not distant nor far.
A hand to hold, a steady gaze,
A presence that whispers, "It's okay to be dazed."
In the warmth of a touch, troubles start to mend,
As the healing journey begins, around the bend.
In the labyrinth of thoughts, where worries reside,
In the ebb and flow of the emotional tide,
There's a sanctuary, a haven of peace,
In the gentle presence, where anxieties cease.
No need for answers, no need to explain,
Just the comfort of knowing, amidst the pain,
That in the stillness, there's a friend by your side,
In the comforting presence, where fears abide.
So let the world whirl, let the storms rage on,
In the quiet companionship, we find we belong.
For in the embrace of a comforting grace,
We discover the strength to embrace each new phase.
In the embrace of a comforting grace,
We find the courage to face,

The trials that come, the battles we fight,
With the comforting presence, everything's right.

The Language of Compassion

In the silent spaces between our words,
Where empathy dwells, and kindness stirs,
There lies a language beyond all tongues,
A tender dialect where healing runs.
It speaks in whispers, soft and kind,
A symphony of hearts, deeply entwined,
In every glance, in every touch,
It conveys the depths of care, oh so much.
It knows no boundaries, nor divides,
It crosses cultures, it unites all sides,
In moments dark, it shines its light,
A beacon of hope in the deepest night.
The language of compassion, gentle and true,
Speaks volumes in what it doesn't construe,
In the warmth of a smile, the grasp of a hand,
It tells stories of love, where souls understand.
It hears the unspoken, feels the unsaid,
In the tears we shed, in the fears we dread,
It offers solace, it brings release,
A balm for the weary, a moment of peace.
It bridges chasms, it mends the fray,
In the brokenness, it finds a way,
To stitch together what's torn apart,
And heal the wounds of the human heart.
So let us speak this language, clear and bright,
With open arms and hearts alight,
For in the embrace of compassion's grace,
We find the beauty of the human race.

Finding Refuge

In the quiet chambers of the heart's retreat,
Where shadows linger and fears find their seat,
There lies a path, obscured by doubt's deceit,
Where seeking souls find solace, bittersweet.
In whispered halls where secrets softly spill,
A sanctuary awaits, tranquil and still,
Where burdens shed their weight, where hearts fulfill,
And weary wanderers find refuge, until
The tender hands of healing gently reach,
To mend the broken fragments, to teach
The art of letting go, to find release,
In vulnerability, in trust, in peace.
With words like gentle rain, they softly guide,
Through labyrinthine depths, they do abide,
To unravel threads of anguish deep inside,
And in their wisdom, wounded souls confide.
With patience, like the steady tide's embrace,
They listen to the echoes of our grace,
They hold the fragments of our fractured space,
And guide us through the darkness, to the place
Where light begins to pierce the heavy veil,
Where hope's soft whisper weaves its gentle tale,
And in the sanctuary, we find the trail
That leads us back to where our spirits sail.
In the refuge of their care, we find
The courage to unravel, to unbind
The knots of pain that once ensnared our mind,
And in their guidance, solace we do find.
So here, within this haven, we begin
The journey of healing, where we've been

Embraced by hands that hold, hearts that have seen
The beauty in our brokenness, serene.
For in the arms of those who understand,
We find the strength to rise, to take a stand,
To walk the path with purpose, hand in hand,
And in their refuge, we reclaim the land.

Voices of Encouragement

In the quiet depths where shadows dwell,
Amid the echoes of my own private hell,
There comes a whisper, soft and clear,
A voice of encouragement, drawing near.
From friends, from kin, from mentors wise,
Their words like stars in the midnight skies,
They weave a tapestry, vibrant and bright,
Guiding me through the darkest night.
"Courage, dear heart," their voices say,
"Though storms may rage, you'll find your way.
Within you lies a strength untold,
A flame of hope that cannot be controlled."
With every word, a seed is sown,
In the fertile soil of my soul, it's grown,
A garden of resilience, blooming strong,
Fueled by the chorus of their song.
Through valleys low and mountains high,
Their voices lift me to the sky,
They hold my hand, they dry my tears,
And chase away my darkest fears.
In their words, I find a sanctuary,
A refuge from life's uncertainty,
For in their presence, I am free,
To embrace the person, I long to be.
So let us raise our voices high,
And sing the song of unity,
For in our words, we hold the key,
To unlock the doors of possibility.
With voices of encouragement, we stand,
A beacon of light in a troubled land,

Together, we rise, together, we soar,
Guided by the love that we adore.
In the symphony of kindness, we find,
The power to heal, the strength to shine,
For in the chorus of our shared refrain,
We discover that we are not alone again.

Through the Storm

In the heart's tempest, where shadows loom tall,
And whispers of doubt in the mind start to call,
In the depths of despair, where darkness prevails,
And the weight of the world seems too heavy to scale.
Through the storm, we journey, battered and worn,
But within the chaos, a flicker is born.
A light in the distance, steady and bright,
Guiding us forward through the darkest of nights.
In the arms of loved ones, we find our retreat,
A sanctuary of solace where fears can retreat.
Their presence a beacon, unwavering, true,
Their love like a lifeline, pulling us through.
Through the storm, we discover the strength we possess,
A resilience that rises, despite the duress.
For in facing the tempest, we learn to believe,
In the power of hope, and the courage to grieve.
Through the storm, we find companionship's grace,
A refuge of understanding in each other's embrace.
Through tears and through laughter, we weather the squall,
Together, unbroken, we rise, and we fall.
For in unity's embrace, there lies our might,
In the bonds that endure through the darkest of nights.
Through the storm, we emerge, stronger than before,
With hearts full of courage, and spirits that soar.
And though clouds may linger, and shadows may roam,
We walk hand in hand, finding our way home.
For in the warmth of connection, we find our true form,
Guided by love, through the fiercest of storms.

The Gift of Presence

In the stillness of the darkest night,
When shadows dance and fears take flight,
There blooms a gift, pure and rare,
A presence that whispers, "I am there."
In the depths of sorrow, where silence reigns,
Amidst the echoes of heartaches and pains,
There shines a light, steady and strong,
A beacon of hope when everything's gone wrong.
It's the touch of a hand, warm and kind,
A gentle reminder, you're not left behind.
In the embrace of a friend, words unspoken,
A sanctuary of love, a promise unbroken.
Through the tempests of doubt and despair,
Through the trials that burden and wear,
There walks a companion, steadfast and true,
A soul who stays, no matter what you're going through.
Their presence, a balm to a wounded heart,
A refuge from the storms that tear apart.
In their eyes, you find solace and grace,
A mirror reflecting the beauty of your own face.
They listen with ears attuned to your sighs,
They hold space for your tears, your fears, your cries.
With empathy as their guiding light,
They navigate the shadows, banishing the night.
Their love, a river that flows endlessly,
A source of strength, a sanctuary, a key.
To unlock the chambers where healing begins,
To mend the broken pieces, to soothe the wounds within.
For in their presence, you find your voice,
In their embrace, you make the choice,

To rise from the ashes, to stand tall and strong,
To reclaim your spirit, where you truly belong.
Their unwavering support, a beacon of hope,
In the vastness of darkness, they help you cope.
With every heartbeat, with every breath,
They offer the gift of presence, beyond life and death.
So, cherish those souls who walk by your side,
In the valleys of sorrow, in the highs and the lows of the tide.
For in their presence, you find the key,
To unlock the door to your destiny.
And when the storms rage and the night grows long,
Remember the gift of presence, forever strong.
For love and empathy, in their purest essence,
Illuminate the path to healing and transcendence.

The Silent Call

In the quiet depths where shadows dwell,
A soul contends, a silent spell,
Bound by chains of doubt and fear,
The heart whispers, yet no one hears.
In the labyrinth of the mind's terrain,
A solitary figure walks in pain,
Beneath the weight of unseen walls,
Echoes linger, silent calls.
Hesitation, a familiar friend,
Like tendrils creeping, without end,
A prisoner of doubt, a captive of fright,
In the darkest hour, veiled from sight.
The silent call, a muted plea,
Lost in the void, yearning to be free,
A symphony of whispers, unheard cries,
In the depths of sorrow, where silence lies.
The heart, a chamber of secrets kept,
Where shadows dance, where dreams are wept,
But in the silence, a flicker of light,
A whisper stirring, breaking the night.
For in the stillness, courage awakes,
A dormant ember, a soul that shakes,
With trembling hands and faltering breath,
The silent call defies death.
With each step, the chains grow light,
As courage kindles, ignites the night,
The journey daunting, the path unsure,
But within the silence, a soul endures.
Through valleys deep and mountains high,
The silent call dares to defy,

The shackles of fear, the bonds of doubt,
As whispers rise, the silence shouts.
For in the act of reaching out,
A heart finds solace, casts off doubt,
In the embrace of understanding eyes,
The silent call begins to rise.
No longer alone, no longer confined,
In the tapestry of souls, the heart entwined,
With each word spoken, each tear shed,
The silent call finds voice instead.
And so, dear soul, if ever you find,
Your spirit burdened, your heart confined,
Remember the power that lies within,
To break the silence, to let light in.
For in the depths where shadows dwell,
The silent call has a tale to tell,
Of courage found, of fears unbound,
In the silent call, true strength is found.

The Silent Call

In the still of night,
Silent cries echo within,
Fear holds back the words.
Heart heavy with doubt,
Whispers lost in the shadows,
Hesitation reigns.
Lingering shadows,
Dancing 'round the edges, dark,
Where light fears to tread.
Invisible chains,
Binding words to trembling lips,
Silence stifles hope.
Yet within the void,
A glimmer of courage stirs,
Breaking through the fear.
A single heartbeat,
A silent call to the soul,
Yearning to be heard.
Courage finds its voice,
A trembling whisper escapes,
Breaking through the dark.
In the quietude,
A new strength begins to rise,
Echoes of resolve.
With each spoken word,
A bridge across the abyss,
Connection restored.
The silent call fades,
Replaced by the song of hope,
Breaking through the night.

Transformation blooms,
In the spaces between breaths,
Courage finds its wings.
And in reaching out,
A hand extended in trust,
Light breaks through the clouds.
For in the silence,
Lies the power to be heard,
The silent call fades.

Section 7: Stigma and Breaking Barriers

In Section 7 of "Whispers of the Soul: A Poetry Anthology on Mental Health and Well-being," Ismael S. Rodriguez Jr. stands as the solitary voice, weaving a poignant narrative that confronts the pervasive stigma surrounding mental health. Through his evocative verses, Ismael delves deep into the complexities of societal perceptions, illuminating the barriers that hinder open discussions and compassionate understanding of mental illness. With raw honesty and unwavering courage, his poetry unveils the hidden struggles endured by those grappling with mental health challenges, urging readers to confront preconceived notions and embrace empathy as a pathway to healing.

Ismael's poetry serves as a beacon of hope, challenging readers to break free from the shackles of stigma and discrimination. His words resonate with authenticity, offering solace to individuals who may feel isolated in their experiences. By shedding light on the human aspect of mental health, Ismael fosters a sense of solidarity and belonging, encouraging readers to confront their own biases and cultivate a culture of acceptance and support. Through his unwavering advocacy, Ismael invites us to embark on a transformative journey of introspection and collective action, where compassion and understanding serve as guiding principles in the quest for mental health equity and inclusion.

Breaking the Silence

In shadows, whispers linger,
Veiled truths and hidden pain,
A symphony of muted cries,
Within hearts, a tempest's reign.
The weight of words unspoken,
Anchors dragging souls below,
Yet hope resides in vulnerability,
Where healing seeds begin to grow.
Break the chains of isolation,
Let empathy be our guide,
Speak of battles fought within,
And the tears we've tried to hide.
For silence is a cruel companion,
Feeding on our darkest fears,
But when voices rise together,
A chorus of resilience appears.
Let us weave a tapestry of courage,
Threads of empathy and grace,
Where stigma crumbles into dust,
And acceptance finds its rightful place.
So, let the winds carry our stories,
Across valleys, mountains, and seas,
Breaking the silence, one word at a time,
For in vulnerability, we find our keys.
Speak, dear heart, without restraint,
For your truth is a beacon of light,
And together, we'll shatter the silence,
Guided by compassion's unwavering might.

Beyond Labels

In whispered corners, names are stitched like seams,
A tapestry of judgments tightly spun,
Yet souls defy the boxes, break their themes.
They brand us with their words, their rigid schemes,
Reducing vibrant lives to just "someone,"
In whispered corners, names are stitched like seams.
"Depressed," "anxious," "broken"—harsh extremes,
Yet hidden strength emerges with the sun,
Yet souls defy the boxes, break their themes.
We wear our labels like ill-fitting dreams,
But deeper truths lie waiting to be spun,
In whispered corners, names are stitched like seams.
See past the surface, where the river gleams,
Each heart a universe, its battles won,
Yet souls defy the boxes, break their themes.
So let us shed these words, these binding streams,
Embrace the messy, fractured, flawed, and spun,
In whispered corners, names are stitched like seams,
Yet souls defy the boxes, break their themes.

Invisible Battles

In the shadows, they
    fight battles unseen by eyes,
    invisible wars.
    Minds a battlefield,
    thoughts like arrows piercing through,
    seeking peace within.
    Each breath a struggle,
    tides of emotion crashing,
    silent screams echo.
    Smiles like armor worn,
    hiding scars that none can see,
    camouflaged in light.
    Invisible wars,
    fought within the depths of self,
    courage amidst fear.
    Whispers in the dark,
    echoes of relentless doubt,
    inner demons rage.
    Yet in quiet strength,
    resilience finds its footing,
    amidst the chaos.
    For every sunrise,
    brings a chance for renewal,
    hope's eternal flame.
    Invisible battles,
    etched in hearts, eternally,
    warriors within.

Judgment's Weight

In shadows deep, where whispers coil,
The weight of judgment takes its toll,
A burden borne by fragile souls,
Who grapple with the tempest's toil.
Within their minds, a storm unfolds,
The tempest's rage, relentless, wild,
As eyes upon them cast their mold,
And cruel tongues weave a web defiled.
Stigma's chains, unyielding, tight,
Constrict the heart, extinguish light.
They walk a path both steep and steeped,
In expectations, heavy, cold,
Their steps encased in iron mold,
As silent battles rage, unwept.
The world, unkind, its verdict swept,
Across their weary hearts, it scorns,
And every tear they've ever kept,
Becomes a thorn, a wound reborn.
Stigma's chains, unyielding, tight,
Constrict the heart, extinguish light.
Yet hidden strength resides within,
A quiet flame that flickers still,
Defying darkness, pain, and ill,
They rise, though bruised, their hearts akin.
For every scar, a tale begins,
Of resilience, courage, grace,
And though the world may judge and spin,
They find their solace in that space.
Stigma's chains, unyielding, tight,
Constrict the heart, extinguish light.

So let us lift our voices high,
Speak truth to silence, break the chains,
Embrace compassion's healing rains,
And see beyond the mask, the lie.
For judgment's weight need not belie
The worth of souls that strive to heal,
To find their place beneath the sky,
Where empathy and love reveal.
Stigma's chains, unyielding, tight,
Constrict the heart, extinguish light.
In unity, we'll redefine,
The measure of a life well-lived,
Not by the judgments harshly given,
But by the kindness we consign.
Let empathy and grace align,
To lift the burden, ease the plight,
And in compassion's light, we find,
The strength to bear judgment's weight.

Shattered Stereotypes

In the garden of minds,
Stereotypes wilt and fade,
Truth blooms, radiant.
Whispers in the wind,
Stereotypes shattered, lost,
Voices rise, unbound.
Labels fall like leaves,
Mental landscapes painted new,
Colors of the soul.
Strength in vulnerability,
Courage in the face of doubt,
Resilience shines bright.
Each story unfolds,
Unique paths through stormy seas,
Mental waves embraced.
In shattered silence,
Echoes of humanity,
Resilience thrives.
Diverse tapestry,
Threads of hope, woven with care,
Stereotypes fray.
Embrace the mosaic,
Beauty in diversity,
Stereotypes shattered.

Behind the Mask

In shadows deep, where secrets softly lie,
A mask adorns the face, a silent guise,
Concealing storms that rage, unseen, inside,
Where teardrops fall like rain from hidden skies.
Behind the mask, a soul in quiet pain,
Enduring battles fought in solitude,
Yet smiles adorn the face, though hearts may strain,
To shield the world from glimpses of its mood.
But oh, beneath the surface, rivers flow,
Emotions swirl like currents deep and wide,
Yearning for solace, longing to bestow
The truth that lurks behind the mask we hide.
So let us seek to see beyond the face,
And offer love and understanding's grace.

Finding Light in the Shadows

In the quiet corners of despair,
    Where shadows cling to wounded hearts,
    A fragile ember dares to flare,
    Seeking solace in the darkest arts.

I. The Veil of Night

The veil of night descends, profound,
Yet whispers weave a fragile thread,
Guiding lost souls toward higher ground,
Where hope's faint glow is gently spread.

II. The Silent Witnesses

Amidst the shadows, silent witnesses stand,
Their eyes reflecting fractured dreams,
They know the weight of judgment's hand,
Yet offer solace in their silent streams.

III. The Resilient Bloom

A flower blooms where shadows creep,
Its petals forged from tears unspoken,
Roots anchored deep, resilience runs deep,
Defying stigma, hearts remain unbroken.

IV. The Kindred Light

In shared vulnerability, a light ignites,
A beacon passed from hand to hand,
Community gathers, hearts take flight,
Together, they weave a stronger strand.

V. Dawn's Promise

As dawn approaches, shadows wane,
Hope's chorus rises, steadfast and bright,
For in unity, we find strength to sustain,
And light emerges from the darkest night.

Voices Unheard

Listen closely to the silence, the space between breaths,
Beneath hums an ache of voices unheard, repressed,
Stigmatized stories yearning to find release,
No peace found until all can speak their truth expressed.
In forgotten corners, shadows linger and grow,
Silent burdens weighing heavy on the mind and soul,
Listen closely to the silence, the space between breaths,
Hear the whispers of those left shivering in the cold.
Society's judgment has shackled them cruelly,
Ashamed to share their struggles openly and freely,
Beneath hums an ache of voices unheard, repressed,
Longing for compassionate ears to truly see.
Too long have they endured quietly in fear,
Feeling like pariahs, "crazy", isolated, drear,
Stigmatized stories yearning to find release,
Seeking understanding allies to hold them dear.
So let us amplify the voices in the void,
And create spaces of empathy unalloyed,
No peace found until all can speak their truth expressed,
Where mental health challenges are not employed.
As reasons to shun or judge another's worth,
But seen as human experiences here on Earth,
Listen closely to the silence, the space between breaths,
And honor their resilience, pain, sorrow and mirth.
For every voice deserves to be wholly heard,
Accepted, included, held onto every word,
Beneath hums an ache of voices unheard, repressed,
But together, with compassion, stigma is deterred.
So let us break the silence and embrace each mind,
Fighting for a world more inclusive and kind,

Stigmatized stories yearning to find release,
Where none feel alone, and all belong combined.
No peace found until all can speak their truth expressed,
And find open arms after being long oppressed.

A New Narrative

In a world where shadows lift,
And light floods in to heal each rift,
A vision forms of minds set free,
From stigma's chains and secrecy.
No more must people hide in shame,
Or feel they are the ones to blame,
For struggles born of chemistry,
And wounds that mar their history.
Instead, compassion paves the way,
For those in pain to have their say,
Empowered to reach out for aid,
Without the fear of being betrayed.
By judgment harsh or labels cruel,
No ridicule for fighting duels,
With inner demons, scars unseen,
On battlefields where they careen.
Alone no more, they find support,
In others who know well their sort,
Of journey long on paths unmarked,
With burdens often borne so stark.
Yet in this world of open hearts,
And minds that strive to play their parts,
The dialogue at last can shift,
To honoring each person's gift.
Of resilience, strength to rise,
Above the pain, beyond the lies,
That whispered they were not enough,
Or that their road was just too tough.
To heal, to grow, to thrive anew,
This vision offers hope imbued,

With change that lets the light break through,
The clouds of stigma misconstrued.
A new narrative then takes hold,
Where stories once untold are told,
And met with grace and empathy,
For every mind fights secretly.
Some battle others cannot see,
But here, no shame will ever be,
Attached to those who bravely face,
Their struggles with unending grace.
Instead, support and care abound,
And hope eternal can be found,
In hands outstretched and open minds,
Where judgment fades and love aligns.
This world imagined beckons bright,
With promise that we all can fight,
For change that lets each voice be heard,
And minds find freedom, spirits stirred.
To seek the help they need to heal,
Without the fear of things concealed,
A new narrative born of hope,
That offers all the chance to cope.
And thrive beyond the darkest night,
Embraced by empathy's warm light.

Compassion's Embrace

In the depths of darkness, when the mind's awhirl
        With storms of anguish, a tempestuous swirl
        Of thoughts that batter, feelings that assail
        The soul that's lost and wandering the gale
        A light appears, a beacon in the night
        A hand outstretched, a presence warm and bright
        Compassion's touch, a balm to soothe the pain
        A listening ear, a heart that shares the strain
        For in our struggles, we are not alone
        Though isolation chills us to the bone
        And whispers lies that no one understands
        The heavy burdens borne by weary hands
        But there are those who've walked a similar path
        Who know the taste of sorrow's bitter wrath
        And in their eyes, a glimmer of hope shines
        A recognition, a bond that intertwines
        For empathy's the bridge that spans the gap
        Between two souls, a connection to unwrap
        The gift of being seen, heard and held dear
        When shadows loom and inner demons' jeer
        To have another say "I'm here with you"
        "You're not alone, I'll help you make it through"
        Can be the lifeline that a soul requires
        To find the strength to face their hidden fires
        And rise above the ashes of despair,
        Knowing they have someone who deeply cares,
        Who listens without judgment or disdain,
        But seeks to understand, to ease the pain,
        By offering a space to be authentic,
        To share the burdens, be they large or quick,

And in that space of openness and trust,
The seeds of healing start to break the crust.
Of isolation, shame and silent suffering,
And in compassion's light, they start uncovering,
The strength within to face another day,
To slowly find a new and brighter way,
With someone by their side who truly sees,
The beauty in their scars and weary pleas,
And cherishes the courage it requires,
To bare one's soul and all that it desires.
For in the end, we all need someone's grace,
To lift us up from sorrow's dark embrace,
To be the mirror that reflects our worth,
When we've forgotten all our light and mirth,
Compassion's touch can be the catalyst,
That sparks the change, the healing to enlist,
And empathy's the salve that soothes the burn,
Of wounds that fester, scars we try to spurn.
So let us be the ones to take a stand,
To extend our hearts and lend a hand,
To those who struggle silent in the night,
And offer them a glimmer of respite,
By listening with patience, seeking to discern,
The stories etched in every twist and turn,
Of their unique and precious tapestry,
And honoring the strength in vulnerability.
For when we dare to meet them where they are,
And walk beside them, whether near or far,
We give the gift of hope and validation,
And help to ease the sting of isolation,
Together we can face the darkest storms,
And find the light that heals and transforms,

For in compassion's warm and tender hold,
The human spirit shines like purest gold.

Unraveling the Mask

In the dim-lit chambers of the mind,
    Where shadows dance and whispers bind,
    A mask is worn, a facade displayed,
    To cloak the turmoil, the dues unpaid.
    Behind the guise of smiles bright,
    Lies a world engulfed in endless night.
    Each laugh a thread, each grin a knot,
    Concealing battles that time forgot.
    The mask, a shield, a fortress tall,
    Hides the cracks, the tears that fall.
    But beneath the layers, a soul cries out,
    Longing to shed the veils of doubt.
    For in the silence of the soul's embrace,
    Lies the courage to reveal its face.
    To peel away the layers, one by one,
    And stand unveiled beneath the sun.
    To let the wounds breathe, to let them heal,
    To embrace the scars, to know they're real.
    For in vulnerability, strength is found,
    As walls crumble to the ground.
    No more the need to pretend or fake,
    No more the burden of hearts that ache.
    For in unraveling the mask we wear,
    Lies the freedom to be truly fair.
    To embrace the flaws, the scars, the pain,
    And dance in the light of truth regained.
    For authenticity, oh sweet release,
    Brings solace, brings comfort, brings inner peace.
    So let us shed the masks we wear,
    And let our truths be known, laid bare.

For in the unraveling, we find our might,
And reclaim the beauty of our inner light.

Bridges of Understanding

Across the chasm, wide and deep,
Where shadows linger, secrets keep,
There lie the bridges, strong and true,
Connecting hearts, both old and new.
Beneath the weight of heavy skies,
Where doubts and fears in darkness rise,
The bridges stand, a beacon bright,
Guiding souls through the darkest night.
Each plank a story, each beam a dream,
Built on hope's resilient gleam,
They span the gap, they bridge the space,
With threads of empathy and grace.
Through valleys deep and mountains tall,
They echo whispers, hear the call,
Of those who journey, lost in mist,
Seeking solace, seeking to exist.
They carry tales of pain and sorrow,
Of dreams deferred and hopes tomorrow,
But also, songs of love and laughter,
Of dreams pursued and futures after.
With every step, with every stride,
They weave together, side by side,
The fabric of humanity,
In shared embrace, in unity.
For on these bridges, hearts collide,
In moments pure, with nothing to hide,
In understanding, we find our worth,
In empathy, we heal the earth.
So let us build these bridges wide,
With beams of love and peace inside,

And walk together, hand in hand,
Towards a world where all can stand.
For in the bridges of understanding,
Lies the power of rebranding,
The narrative of mental health,
With compassion as our greatest wealth.

Section 8: The Beauty of Imperfection

Section 8, "The Beauty of Imperfection," celebrates the inherent beauty found within the complexities of human existence, with Ismael S Rodriguez Jr's poignant verses serving as the focal point. Through his introspective reflections, Ismael invites readers on a soul-stirring exploration of self-acceptance and the embracing of imperfections as a fundamental aspect of the human experience. His poems resonate with a profound sense of authenticity, revealing the transformative power of vulnerability and the courage it takes to embrace one's flaws. Ismael's evocative imagery and lyrical prose remind us that our imperfections are not merely blemishes but rather unique brushstrokes that contribute to the masterpiece of our lives.

Within this section, Ismael's poetry acts as a beacon of light, guiding readers towards a deeper understanding of self-love and acceptance. Through his verses, he emphasizes the beauty found in embracing our scars and vulnerabilities, encouraging readers to recognize that true beauty lies not in perfection, but in the authenticity of our flaws. Ismael's words serve as a gentle reminder that our imperfections are what make us beautifully human, and it is through accepting them that we can embark on a journey of self-discovery and genuine connection with ourselves and others. As readers immerse themselves in Ismael's heartfelt verses, they are inspired to embrace their own imperfections with grace and compassion, ultimately discovering the profound beauty that lies within.

Portrait of a Wabi-Sabi Sou

In the cracks and crevices of time-worn face,
  A tapestry of stories can be traced.
  Each line a brush stroke, painted by life's hand,
  A weathered landscape, beautifully unplanned.
  Perfection's facade, a crumbling veneer,
  Beneath which wabi-sabi truths appear.
  In flaws and scars, a deeper grace resides,
  Where beauty's essence patiently abides,
  Awaiting those with eyes that truly see
  The perfect imperfections that set souls free.
  The winding path of life, a journey long,
  With twists and turns, a melody of song.
  Each step a dance, a movement full of grace,
  Though stumbles mark the rhythm, leave their trace.
  Yet in the missteps, wisdom's seeds are sown,
  And character's rich hues are gently grown.
  For in the struggles, strength and courage rise,
  And in the falls, the chance to realize
  That every scar and wound that leaves its mark
  Becomes a guiding light, a glowing spark.
  In the wrinkles of a well-worn, aged face,
  A map of memories, time cannot erase.
  Each line a tributary of life's flow,
  A history etched in skin, a tale to know.
  The smoothness of youth, a fleeting phase,
  But depth of spirit, time cannot erase.
  For in the weathered visage, wisdom gleams,
  And in the silver strands, experience beams.
  The wabi-sabi soul embraces change,
  Finds beauty in the aging, the un-strange.

The imperfections that the world may see,
Are but the brushstrokes of authenticity.
The flaws and quirks, the cracks and rough-hewn lines,
Are what make every soul distinctly shine.
In the wabi-sabi heart, there is no shame,
For every scar and fault, there is no blame.
Acceptance reigns, a peace with what is true,
Embracing all the shades of me and you.
For in our imperfections, we are real,
And in our flaws, our humanity we feel.
The wabi-sabi soul is not afraid,
Of time's inevitable, changing raid.
For in the transient nature of all things,
A deeper understanding gently springs.
That life is but a fleeting, precious dance,
And every moment, every circumstance,
Is but a brush stroke on the canvas vast,
A part of the masterpiece, unsurpassed.
So let us celebrate the incomplete,
The beauty in the flawed, the bittersweet.
For in the wabi-sabi way of sight,
There is no wrong or right, just different light.
Each soul a unique portrait, painted true,
In hues and shades of me and shades of you.
So let us honor every crack and line,
And in our flaws, let gentleness entwine.
For in acceptance, there is grace to be,
A love for all the beauty we can't see.
The wabi-sabi soul, a work of art,
Imperfectly perfect, a sacred part.

In Praise of Unfinished Symphonies

In the grand symphony of life, each measure a mystery,
Some notes soar with joy, while others resound with grief.
Yet every chord, every rest, plays a part in the tapestry.
The composition evolves, a work forever in progress,
An opus woven from moments, both bitter and sweet.
In the grand symphony of life, each measure a mystery.
Some phrases are haunting, minor keys that echo sorrow,
While others dance vivace, a vivid, lively motif.
Yet every chord, every rest, plays a part in the tapestry.
At times the tempo drags, a languid, mournful largo,
The melody line falters, uncertain where to proceed.
In the grand symphony of life, each measure a mystery.
But then a new theme emerges, hope's refrain awakens,
The harmony shifts, resilience rising from beneath.
Yet every chord, every rest, plays a part in the tapestry.
In the movements of our lives, we are both composer and song,
Improvising as we go, learning to embrace dissonant keys.
In the grand symphony of life, each measure a mystery.
Though the final notes remain unwritten, a future yet to be,
We play on with courage, add our voices to the symphony.
Yet every chord, every rest, plays a part in the tapestry.
For it's the unresolved cadences, the unfinished refrains,
That give the music depth, make the journey rich and deep.
In the grand symphony of life, each measure a mystery,
Yet every chord, every rest, plays a part in the tapestry.

Ode to Flawed Beauty

Oh, the exquisite grace of imperfection,
The charm that lies within each blemish and scar.
In the tapestry of life, a beautiful reflection,
Of the journey we've traveled, both near and far.
In a world that oft demands a polished veneer,
Let us celebrate the beauty that's raw and real.
For in the cracks and crevices, true character appears,
A testament to the strength of the human ideal.
The scars we bear are stories etched upon our skin,
Chapters of resilience, tales of battles fought.
They are not flaws to hide or imperfections to rescind,
But badges of honor, a map of lessons taught.
In the asymmetry of a crooked smile, a quirky gait,
There is a unique charm that no one can replicate.
It's the distinctive features that make us stand apart,
And add depth and dimension to the beauty of our heart.
The lines that time has carved upon a weathered face,
Are not to be erased or viewed with disdain.
For in each wrinkle, there's a story to embrace,
A life well-lived, a history to sustain.
So let us cast aside the notion of perfection's mold,
And embrace the beauty that's unconventional and bold.
For in our flaws and scars, we find our truth revealed,
A masterpiece of individuality, authentically sealed.
In the mosaic of humanity, each piece is essential,
No matter how chipped, cracked, or differently shaped.
It's the imperfections that make the whole consequential,
A work of art that's beautifully flawed and intricately draped.
So, wear your scars with pride, your blemishes with grace,
For they are the marks of a life embraced.

In the symphony of beauty, each note has its place,
And it's the flaws that make the melody rich and unabased.
Oh, flawed beauty, how we adore and celebrate,
The uniqueness that you bring, the character you create.
For in embracing our imperfections, we truly liberate,
The authentic beauty that resides in each and every state.

Embracing Shadows

In the corners of the soul, where darkness reigns,
    Lurk the shadows, silent whispers, hidden pains.
    They dance in the quiet, unseen by light's embrace,
    Yet within their depths, truths find their space.
    Embracing shadows, we confront the unknown,
    The parts of ourselves, in darkness, we have sown.
    For in the depths of night, where fears reside,
    Lie the keys to understanding, to self-untried.
    These shadows, they are not foes to fight,
    But mirrors reflecting the depths of our plight.
    In their midst, lies the essence of our being,
    A tapestry of scars, wounds, and unseen meaning.
    To deny the shadows is to deny the self,
    To lock away truths in a forgotten shelf.
    Yet in embracing them, we find liberation's key,
    For in shadows lies the path to set us free.
    They whisper tales of resilience, of strength untold,
    In the caverns of darkness, new stories unfold.
    For within every shadow, there lies a spark,
    A glimmer of hope piercing through the dark.
    So let us embrace the shadows, without fear or dread,
    For in their depths lies the wisdom to be fed.
    In integrating them, we find our truest form,
    A symphony of light and shadow, weathering life's storm.

In Praise of Unfinished Stories

In twilight's embrace,
    Unfinished tales whisper soft,
    Promises of dawn.
    Each step, a brushstroke,
    Painting dreams upon the sky,
    In colors unseen.
    Unwritten chapters,
    Dance in the shadows of time,
    Yearning to unfold.
    The winding pathways,
    Echo with untold secrets,
    Lost in misty veils.
    Unfinished stories,
    Threads of possibility,
    Weave through the unknown.
    In the silent pause,
    Lies the beauty of beginnings,
    Unfolding, untamed.
    Embrace the journey,
    For in its twists and turns lie
    Truths yet to be found.
    Let go of the end,
    Embrace the dance of the now,
    Where stories take flight.
    In praise of the incomplete,
    The beauty of the journey,
    Where endings begin.

Dancing in the Rain

In the midst of life's tempests, we stand,
Battered by winds, drenched by rain's command.
Yet, in the chaos, a melody we hear,
A song of resilience, ringing clear.
Dancing in the rain, we find our grace,
Amidst the downpour, we embrace.
Each drop a rhythm, each puddle a stage,
We twirl and whirl, regardless of age.
For in adversity's fierce, relentless roar,
We discover strength we never knew before.
Our spirits rise, unbroken, unbowed,
As we dance with courage, head unbowed.
In every droplet, a lesson learned,
In every downpour, a bridge we've earned.
For storms may rage, and skies may weep,
But in the dance, our souls find peace to keep.
With every step, we defy the dark,
With every movement, we leave our mark.
For joy resides in the heart's refrain,
When we find solace in dancing in the rain.
So let the storm clouds gather high,
Let thunder echo through the sky.
We'll dance with joy, we'll dance with pain,
For in the rain, our spirits reign.
And when the storm at last does pass,
We'll treasure memories of rain-soaked grass.
For in the dance, we've learned to thrive,
And find the beauty in being alive.

The Patchwork Quilt of Self

In the quiet corner of the soul's abode,
There lies a quilt, a story yet untold.
Threads of life, both bright and dim,
Woven together, a tapestry within.
Each patch, a tale of days gone by,
Stitched with laughter, stitched with sighs.
In colors vibrant, in hues subdued,
The patchwork quilt of self-imbued.
Here, a patch of joy, stitched with glee,
A memory of moments wild and free.
There, a tear-stained cloth, weathered and worn,
A testament to the storms we've borne.
In every seam, a whisper of the past,
A journey etched in fabric that will last.
For every stitch, a lesson learned,
A wisdom gained; a bridge discerned.
The quilt of self, a mosaic rare,
A symphony of hopes, a solace shared.
With flaws and triumphs, it comes alive,
A testament to the human spirit's drive.
For in its patches, we find our truth,
The essence of our days, the dreams of youth.
And though it may fray, and though it may tear,
The quilt of self, we'll always wear.
So let us cherish each patch we hold,
For in its fibers, our stories unfold.
In the patchwork quilt of self, we find,
The beauty of a life, intertwined.

Unwritten Poems

In silence, there are stories left untold,
A universe of words that lie unsaid.
The beauty of the mysteries they hold,
Are like unwritten poems in the head.
Each pause, each breath, each moment that goes by,
Is laden with the weight of tales unheard.
The unspoken emotions, dreams that fly,
Are poems in the heart, without a word.
There's beauty in the secrets that we keep,
The stories that we hold within our core.
They are the seeds of poems, buried deep,
Awaiting for the right moment to soar.
Embrace the unknown, the tales untold,
For in the unspoken, beauty unfolds.

Blossoming in Brokenness

In the garden of the soul, amidst the thorns,
Where shadows linger and silence mourns,
There blooms a flower, fragile and small,
Blossoming in brokenness, standing tall.
Petals scarred, yet each one a story,
Of trials faced, of battles gory,
Roots entwined with shards of pain,
Watered by tears that fell like rain.
In the depths of despair, where darkness reigns,
The seed of resilience quietly sustains,
For in the depths of every shattered dream,
Lies the birthplace of a resilient gleam.
Through cracks in the heart, light seeps in,
Igniting the spirit, ready to begin,
A journey of healing, of growth, of grace,
Where brokenness becomes a sacred space.
With each passing storm, the flower bends,
But never breaks, never surrenders, never ends,
For within its essence lies a strength untold,
A testament to the resilience it holds.
And as the sun rises, painting the sky,
The broken bloom unfurls, reaching high,
A beacon of hope, amidst the strife,
A symbol of beauty, forged from life.
So let us honor the scars that we bear,
For they are the badges of battles we dare,
And in our brokenness, we find our might,
Blossoming in beauty, in the darkest night.

The Art of Self-Compassion

In the quiet chambers of the soul,
Where shadows dance and doubts take toll,
There lies a truth we often ignore,
A whisper of solace we've yet to explore.
In moments of darkness, when skies turn gray,
And echoes of failure cloud our way,
There blooms a seed, so tender and true,
The art of self-compassion, awaiting its due.
Like a gentle breeze on a stormy night,
It cradles our wounds, brings healing light,
With hands of kindness, soft and warm,
It soothes the soul in the midst of the storm.
In the mirror's gaze, where flaws reside,
Let compassion bloom, let love abide,
For within these lines and scars we see,
The beauty of our humanity.
Speak to yourself with a gentle voice,
For you are worthy, you have a choice,
To embrace the depths of your own grace,
And find strength in this sacred space.
Treat yourself as you would a friend,
With tenderness that knows no end,
For in the art of self-compassion, we find,
The courage to heal, the power to shine.
So let kindness guide each step you take,
And let love be the path you make,
For in the embrace of your own affection,
Lies the true essence of perfection.

Finding Beauty in the Unseen

In the cracks and crevices of life's façade,
There lies a beauty that often goes untrod.
It's not the postcard-perfect scenes,
But the imperfect, the unseen.
Amidst the mundane, the everyday routine,
There are moments of wonder, if you look between.
In the rusty gates and weathered walls,
Beauty waits, its silent call.
It's in the dandelion pushing through concrete,
Or the spider's web, glistening, a marvel discreet.
The dance of dust motes in a sunbeam,
A secret world, a glimpse of dream.
There's beauty in the wrinkles of a smile well-worn,
In the scars that tell stories, a life adorned.
It's in the laughter lines and crow's feet,
Testaments to joy, a life replete.
The unseen symphony of a bustling street,
Footsteps, chatter, and heartbeats,
Creating a rhythm, a life force's dance,
Beauty in the ordinary happenstance.
It's in the morning dew on a blade of grass,
Or the pattern of raindrops on a window glass.
The swirling steam rising from a cup of tea,
A moment of beauty, a fleeting reverie.
So, look beyond the surface, the mainstream's gaze,
And find the beauty in the unseen, the unsung praise.
For in the cracks and shadows, life's true art,
Lies waiting to be discovered, to touch your heart.
The capacity to wonder, to find awe in the small,
Is a gift that enriches, a beauty to enthrall.

So, embrace the unseen, the overlooked, the everyday,
And let the beauty of the mundane take your breath away.

Chiaroscuro of the Self

In the canvas of the soul, a masterpiece unfolds,
    Brushstrokes of light and shadow, a story to be told.
    The interplay of brightness and darkness, a dance,
    Creating depth and dimension, a beautiful happenstance.
    The light within, a radiant glow,
    Illuminating strengths, talents, a beautiful show.
    It shines through acts of kindness, compassion, and love,
    Reflecting the best of oneself, like a peaceful dove.
    Yet shadows too, play their part,
    Adding depth, complexity, a work of art.
    The darkness of fears, doubts, and pain,
    Contrasting with the light, like a gentle rain.
    It's in the shades of gray, the nuances between,
    That the true self emerges, a sight to be seen.
    The intermingling of light and dark, a subtle hue,
    Revealing the authentic, the real, the true.
    For without the shadows, the light would be flat,
    A one-dimensional image, without contrast, without that.
    It's the interplay of both, the chiaroscuro effect,
    That creates a masterpiece, a self to respect.
    The journey of self-discovery, a painting to create,
    With each brush of experience, a new layer to relate.
    The dance of light and shadow, an evolving art,
    Shaping the canvas of the soul, a beautiful start.
    So, embrace the light, the radiance within,
    But also honor the shadows, the depths therein.
    For it's in the fusion of both, the self comes alive,
    A chiaroscuro masterpiece, a work to thrive.
    The complexities of the self, a beautiful design,
    Illuminated by light, shadowed by the divine.

A work of art, a tapestry to behold,
In the chiaroscuro of the self, a story to be told.

Canvas of Scars

Upon the skin, a map of life,
Scars etched deep, tales of strife.
Each mark, a story to unfold,
Of battles fought, and pains untold.
The jagged lines, a testament,
To resilience, a covenant.
With strength, the body and soul mend,
Healing wounds, a journey to transcend.
In the tapestry of scars, woven tight,
Threads of courage, a beautiful sight.
For every scar, a triumph won,
A testament to endurance, a race well run.
The scars may fade, but the stories stay,
Reminders of the price paid, day by day.
For survival, for growth, for lessons learned,
In the furnace of pain, a spirit earned.
So, wear your scars with pride, a badge of honor,
A canvas of resilience, a silent roar.
For each mark tells a tale of bravery,
Of a soul that refused to bend the knee.
In the patchwork of scars, a quilt of strength,
A testament to the human spirit's length.
For scars are not flaws, but works of art,
Masterpieces etched upon the heart.
They speak of battles won, of demons faced,
Of pain endured, and fears erased.
They are the brushstrokes of a life well-lived,
Of challenges met and hope revived.
So let your scars be a canvas, a story to share,
Of resilience, of courage, of a soul laid bare.

For in the tapestry of marks, a beauty resides,
A testament to the strength that abides.

Conclusion:

In the gentle cadence of Ismael S. Rodriguez Jr.'s verses, we find solace and resonance, woven delicately into the fabric of our shared human experience. Through the pages of this anthology, Ismael's words serve as a beacon, illuminating the often-obscured paths of mental health and well-being. His poetry, a testament to the complexities of the soul, invites readers to embark on a journey of introspection and understanding, where vulnerability is embraced, and healing is an ever-present possibility.

As the only poet within this anthology, Ismael's voice resonates with sincerity and depth, offering insights that transcend the boundaries of language and culture. His verses traverse the spectrum of human emotion, from the depths of despair to the heights of hope, mirroring the intricate tapestry of the human psyche. Through his poetry, Ismael extends a hand of empathy to those navigating the labyrinth of mental health, reminding us that our struggles do not define us, but rather, they shape the contours of our resilience.

In the tender embrace of Ismael's poetry, we find refuge from the tumult of our inner worlds, where the echoes of our fears and aspirations mingle harmoniously with the whispers of self-discovery. His words serve as a gentle reminder that in moments of darkness, there exists the promise of dawn, and within the labyrinth of our minds, the seeds of healing take root. Through his unwavering sincerity and vulnerability, Ismael invites us to confront our shadows with compassion and to embrace the beauty found within the depths of our imperfections.

As we bid farewell to these pages, may we carry with us the enduring wisdom of Ismael S. Rodriguez Jr.'s poetry, a beacon of light in times of uncertainty and a testament to the resilience of the human spirit. In the tapestry of our shared experiences, may his words continue to echo, serving as a reminder of the boundless capacity for healing and transformation that resides within each of us.

Ismael S. Rodriguez Jr., also known as The Bulletproof Poet, is a talented and diverse artist, author, and poet of Puerto Rican and Filipino descent. He was born and raised in Philadelphia, PA, and now lives in Oakland Park, FL. Rodriguez has a range of interests and experiences, including serving in the U.S. Navy and being deployed during Desert Storm. Despite facing numerous challenges in his life, including schizophrenia, PTSD, substance abuse, and homelessness, Rodriguez has overcome these obstacles and has been sober for 16 years. He is also actively seeking treatment for his mental and emotional health issues. In addition to his artistic pursuits, Rodriguez is an ordained reverend and practices Grey Witchcraft, Discordianism, and ceremonial magic. His website, https://thebulletproofpoet1.godaddysites.com/home, showcases his poetry, short stories, origami, and more. You can find additional links to his work on his Linktree https://linktr.ee/bulletproofpoet

www.ingramcontent.com/pod-product-compliance
Lightning Source LLC
Chambersburg PA
CBHW061340160726
47995CB00001B/115